Waiting for Christ's Coming

Meditations for Advent, Christmas, & Epiphany

By

Saint John Henry Cardinal Newman

Annotated & Edited by
Cameron M. Thompson, MA, Psy.D.

Published by

Marchese di Carabàs

ISBN: 978-1-7356578-2-0

TABLE OF CONTENTS

ADVENT

Advent—Lauds

En clara vox redarguit.

Hark, a joyful voice is thrilling,
And each dim and winding way
Of the ancient Temple filling;
Dreams, depart! for it is day.

Christ is coming!—from thy bed,
Earth-bound soul, awake and spring,—
With the sun new-risen to shed
Health on human suffering.

Lo! to grant a pardon free,
Comes a willing Lamb from Heaven;
Sad and tearful, hasten we,
One and all, to be forgiven.

Once again He comes in light,
Girding earth with fear and woe;
Lord! be Thou our loving Might,
From our guilt and ghostly foe.

To the Father, and the Son,
And the Spirit, who in Heaven
Ever witness, Three and One,
Praise on earth be ever given.

Worship, a Preparation for Christ's Coming

"Thine eyes shall see the King in his beauty: they shall behold the land that is very far off." Isaiah 33:17

Year after year, as it passes, brings us the same warnings again and again, and none perhaps more impressive than those with which it comes to us at this season. The very frost and cold, rain and gloom, which now befall us, forebode the last dreary days of the world, and in religious hearts raise the thought of them. The year is worn out: spring, summer, autumn, each in turn, have brought their gifts and done their utmost; but they are over, and the end is come. All is past and gone, all has failed, all has sated; we are tired of the past; we would not have the seasons longer; and the austere weather which succeeds, though ungrateful to the body, is in tone with our feelings, and acceptable. Such is the frame of mind which befits the end of the year; and such the frame of mind which comes alike on good and bad at the end of life. The days have come in which they have no pleasure; yet they would hardly be young again, could they be so by wishing it. Life is well enough in its way; but it does not satisfy. Thus the soul is cast forward upon the future, and in proportion as its conscience is clear and its perception keen and true, does it rejoice solemnly that "the night is far spent, the day is at hand," that there are "new heavens and a new earth" to come, though the former are failing; nay, rather that, because they are failing, it will "soon see the King in His beauty," and "behold the land which is very far off." These are feelings for holy men in winter and in age, waiting, in some dejection perhaps, but with comfort on the whole, and calmly though earnestly, for the Advent of Christ.

And such, too, are the feelings with which we now come before Him in prayer day by day. The season is chill and dark, and the breath of the morning is damp, and worshippers are few, but all this befits those who are by profession penitents and mourners, watchers and pilgrims. More dear to them that loneliness, more cheerful that severity, and more bright that gloom, than all those aids and appliances of luxury by which men nowadays attempt to make prayer less disagreeable to them. True faith does not covet comforts. It only complains when it is forbidden to kneel, when it reclines upon cushions, is protected by curtains, and encompassed by warmth. Its only hardship is to be hindered, or to be ridiculed, when it would place itself as a sinner before its Judge. They who realize that awful Day when they shall see Him face to face, whose eyes are as a flame of fire, will as little bargain to pray pleasantly now, as they will think of doing so then.

One year goes and then another, but the same warnings recur. The frost or the rain comes again; the earth is stripped of its brightness; there is nothing to rejoice in. And then, amid this unprofitableness of earth and sky, the well-known words return; the Prophet Isaiah is read; the same Epistle and Gospel, bidding us "awake out of sleep," and welcome Him "that cometh in the Name of the Lord;" the same Collects, beseeching Him to prepare us for judgment. O blessed they who obey these warning voices, and look out for Him whom they have not seen, because they "love His appearing!"

We cannot have fitter reflections at this Season than those which I have entered upon. What may be the destiny of other orders of beings we know not—but this we know to be our own fearful lot, that before us lies a time when we must have the sight of our Maker and Lord face to face. We know not what is reserved for other beings; there may be some, which, knowing nothing of their Maker, are never to be brought before Him. For what we can tell, this may be the case with the brute creation. It may be the law of their nature that they should live and die, or live on an indefinite period, upon the very outskirts of His government, sustained by Him, but never permitted to know or approach Him. But this is not our case. We are destined to come before Him; nay, and to come before Him in judgment; and that on our first meeting; and that suddenly. We are not merely to be rewarded or punished, we are to be judged. Recompense is to come upon our actions, not by a mere general provision or course of nature, as it does at present, but from the Lawgiver Himself in person. We have to stand before His righteous Presence, and that one by one. One by one we shall have to endure His holy and searching eye. At present we are in a world of shadows. What we see is not substantial. Suddenly it will be rent in twain and vanish away, and our Maker will appear. And then, I say, that first appearance will be nothing less than a personal intercourse between the Creator and every creature. He will look on us, while we look on Him.

I need hardly quote any of the numerous passages of Scripture which tell us this, by way of proof; but it may impress the truth of it upon our hearts to do so. We are told then expressly, that good and bad shall see God. On the one hand holy Job says, "Though after my skin worms destroy this body, yet in my flesh shall I see God: whom I shall see for myself, and mine eyes shall behold, and not another." On the other hand unrighteous Balaam says, "I shall see Him, but not now; I shall behold Him, but not nigh; there shall come a Star out of Jacob, and a Sceptre shall rise out of Israel." Christ says to His disciples, "Look up, and lift up your heads, for your redemption draweth nigh;" and to His enemies, "Hereafter ye shall see the Son of man sitting on the right hand of power, and coming in the clouds of heaven." And it is said generally of all men, on the one hand, "Behold He cometh with clouds; and every eye shall see Him, and they also which pierced Him; and all kindreds of the earth shall wail because of Him." And on the other, "When He shall appear, we shall be like Him; for we shall see Him as He is." Again, "Now we see through a glass, darkly; but then face to face:" and again, "They shall see His face; and His Name shall be in their foreheads."[1]

And, as they see Him, so will He see them, for His coming will be to judge them. "We must all appear before the judgment-seat of Christ," says St. Paul. Again, "We shall all stand before the judgment-seat of Christ. For it is written, As I live, saith the Lord, every

---

[1] Job 19:26-27; Numb. 24:17; Luke 21:28; Matt. 26:64; Rev. 1:7; 1 John 3:2; 1 Cor. 13:12; Rev. 22:4

knee shall bow to Me, and every tongue shall confess to God. So then every one of us shall give account of himself to God." And again, "When the Son of man shall come in His glory, and all the holy Angels with Him, then shall He sit upon the throne of His glory. And before Him shall be gathered all nations; and He shall separate them one from another, as a shepherd divideth his sheep from the goats."[2]

Such is our first meeting with our God; and, I say, it will be as sudden as it is intimate. "Yourselves know perfectly," says St. Paul, "that the day of the Lord so cometh as a thief in the night. For when they shall say, Peace and safety, then sudden destruction cometh upon them." This is said of the wicked,—elsewhere He is said to surprise good as well as bad. "While the Bridegroom tarried," the wise and foolish virgins "all slumbered and slept. And at midnight there was a cry made, Behold, the Bridegroom cometh; go ye out to meet Him."[3]

Now, when this state of the case, the prospect which lies before us, is brought home to our thoughts, surely it is one which will lead us anxiously to ask, Is this all that we are told, all that is allowed to us, or done for us? Do we know only this, that all is dark now, and all will be light then; that now God is hidden, and one day will be revealed? that we are in a world of sense, and are to be in a world of spirits? For surely it is our plain wisdom, our bounden duty, to prepare for this great change;— and if so, are any directions, hints, or rules given us *how*

---

[2] 2 Cor. 5:10; Rom. 14:10-12; Matt. 25:31-32
[3] 1 Thess. 5:2-3; Matt. 25:5-6

we are to prepare? "Prepare to meet thy God," "Go ye out to meet Him," is the dictate of natural reason, as well as of inspiration. But *how* is this to be?

Now observe, that it is scarcely a sufficient answer to this question to say that we must strive to obey Him, and so to approve ourselves to Him. This indeed might be enough, were reward and punishment to follow in the mere way of nature, as they do in this world. But, when we come steadily to consider the matter, appearing before God, and dwelling in His presence, is a very different thing from being merely subjected to a system of moral laws, and would seem to require another preparation, a special preparation of thought and affection, such as will enable us to endure His countenance, and to hold communion with Him as we ought. Nay, and, it may be, a preparation of the soul itself for His presence, just as the bodily eye must be exercised in order to bear the full light of day, or the bodily frame in order to bear exposure to the air.

But, whether or not this be safe reasoning, Scripture precludes the necessity of it, by telling us that the Gospel Covenant is intended, among its other purposes, to prepare us for this future glorious and wonderful destiny, the sight of God,—a destiny which, if not most glorious, will be most terrible. And in the worship and service of Almighty God, which Christ and His Apostles have left to us, we are vouchsafed means, both moral and mystical, of approaching God, and gradually learning to bear the sight of Him.

This indeed is the most momentous reason for religious worship, as far as we have grounds for considering it a true one. Men sometimes ask, Why need they *profess* religion? Why need they go to church? Why need they observe certain rites and ceremonies? Why need they watch, pray, fast, and meditate? Why is it not enough to be just, honest, sober, benevolent, and otherwise virtuous? Is not this the true and real worship of God? Is not activity in mind and conduct the most acceptable way of approaching Him? How can they please Him by submitting to certain religious forms, and taking part in certain religious acts? Or if they must do so, why may they not choose their own? Why must they come to church for them? Why must they be partakers in what the Church calls Sacraments? I answer, they must do so, first of all and especially, because God tells them so to do. But besides this, I observe that we see this plain reason why, that they are one day to change their state of being. They are not to be here for ever. Direct intercourse with God on their part now, prayer and the like, may be necessary to their meeting Him suitably hereafter: and direct intercourse on His part with them, or what we call sacramental communion, may be necessary in some incomprehensible way, even for preparing their very nature to bear the sight of Him.

Let us then take this view of religious service; it is "going out to meet the Bridegroom," who, if not seen "in His beauty," will appear in consuming fire. Besides its other momentous reasons, it is a preparation for an awful event, which shall one day be. What it would be to meet Christ at once without preparation, we may learn from what happened even to the Apostles when His glory was suddenly manifested to them. St. Peter said, "Depart from me, for I am a sinful man, O Lord." And St. John, "when he saw Him, fell at His feet as dead."[4]

This being the case, it is certainly most merciful in God to vouchsafe to us the means of preparation, and such means as He has actually appointed. When Moses came down from the Mount, and the people were dazzled at his countenance, he put a veil over it. That veil is so far removed in the Gospel, that we are in a state of preparation for its being altogether removed. We are with Moses in the Mount so far, that we have a sight of God; we are with the people beneath it so far, that Christ does not visibly show Himself. He has put a veil on, and He sits among us silently and secretly. When we approach Him, we know it only by faith; and when He manifests Himself to us, it is without our being able to realize to ourselves that manifestation.

Such then is the spirit in which we should come to all His ordinances, considering them as anticipations and first-fruits of that sight of Him which one day must be. When we kneel down in prayer in private, let us think to ourselves, Thus shall I one day kneel down before His very footstool, in this flesh and this blood of mine; and He will be seated over against me, in flesh and blood also, though divine. I come, with the thought of that awful hour before me, I come to confess my sin to Him now, that He may pardon it then, and I say, "O Lord, Holy God, Holy and Strong, Holy and Immortal, in the hour of death and in the day of judgment, deliver us, O Lord!"

---

[4] Luke 5:8; Rev. 1:17

Again, when we come to church, then let us say: The day will be when I shall see Christ surrounded by His Holy Angels. I shall be brought into that blessed company, in which all will be pure, all bright. I come then to learn to endure the sight of the Holy One and His Servants; to nerve myself for a vision which is fearful before it is ecstatic, and which they only enjoy whom it does not consume. When men in this world have to undergo any great thing, they prepare themselves beforehand, by thinking often of it, and they call this making up their mind. Any unusual trial they thus make familiar to them. Courage is a necessary step in gaining certain goods, and courage is gained by steady thought. Children are scared, and close their eyes, at the vision of some mighty warrior or glorious king. And when Daniel saw the Angel, like St. John, "his comeliness was turned in him into corruption, and he retained no strength."[5] I come then to church, because I am an heir of heaven. It is my desire and hope one day to take possession of my inheritance: and I come to make myself ready for it, and I would not see heaven yet, for I could not bear to see it. I am allowed to be in it without seeing it, that I may learn to see it. And by psalm and sacred song, by confession and by praise, I learn my part.

And what is true of the ordinary services of religion, public and private, holds in a still higher or rather in a special way, as regards the sacramental ordinances of the Church. In these is manifested in greater or less degree, according to the measure of

---

[5] Dan. 10:8

13

each, that Incarnate Saviour, who is one day to be our Judge, and who is enabling us to bear His presence then, by imparting it to us in measure now. A thick black veil is spread between this world and the next. We mortal men range up and down it, to and fro, and see nothing. There is no access through it into the next world. In the Gospel this veil is not removed; it remains, but every now and then marvellous disclosures are made to us of what is behind it. At times we seem to catch a glimpse of a Form which we shall hereafter see face to face. We approach, and in spite of the darkness, our hands, or our head, or our brow, or our lips become, as it were, sensible of the contact of something more than earthly. We know not where we are, but we have been bathing in water, and a voice tells us that it is blood. Or we have a mark signed upon our foreheads, and it spake of Calvary. Or we recollect a hand laid upon our heads, and surely it had the print of nails in it, and resembled His who with a touch gave sight to the blind and raised the dead. Or we have been eating and drinking; and it was not a dream surely, that One fed us from His wounded side, and renewed our nature by the heavenly meat He gave. Thus in many ways He, who is Judge to us, prepares us to be judged —He, who is to glorify us, prepares us to be glorified, that He may not take us unawares; but that when the voice of the Archangel sounds, and we are called to meet the Bridegroom, we may be ready.

Now consider what light these reflections throw upon some remarkable texts in the Epistle to the Hebrews. If we have in the Gospel this supernatural approach to God and to the next world, no wonder that

St. Paul calls it an "enlightening," "a tasting of the heavenly gift," a being "made partaker of the Holy Ghost," a "tasting of the good word of God, and the powers of the world to come." No wonder, too, that utter apostasy after receiving it should be so utterly hopeless; and that in consequence, any profanation of it, any sinning against it, should be so perilous in proportion to its degree. If He, who is to be our Judge, condescend here to manifest Himself to us, surely if that privilege does not fit us for His future glory, it does but prepare us for His wrath.

And what I have said concerning Ordinances, applies still more fully to Holy Seasons, which include in them the celebration of many Ordinances. They are times when we may humbly expect a larger grace, because they invite us especially to the means of grace. This in particular is a time for purification of every kind. When Almighty God was to descend upon Mount Sinai, Moses was told to "sanctify the people," and bid them "wash their clothes," and to "set bounds to them round about"—much more is this a season for "cleansing ourselves from all defilement of the flesh and spirit, perfecting holiness in the fear of God"[6]—a season for chastened hearts and religious eyes; for severe thoughts, and austere resolves, and charitable deeds; a season for remembering what we are and what we shall be. Let us go out to meet Him with contrite and expectant hearts; and though He delays His coming, let us watch for Him in the cold and dreariness which must one day have an end. Attend His summons

---

[6] Exod. 19:10-12. 2 Cor. 12:1

we must, at any rate, when He strips us of the body; let us anticipate, by a voluntary act, what will one day come on us of necessity. Let us wait for Him solemnly, fearfully, hopefully, patiently, obediently; let us be resigned to His will, while active in good works. Let us pray Him ever, to "remember us when He cometh in His kingdom;" to remember all our friends; to remember our enemies; and to visit us according to His mercy here, that He may reward us according to His righteousness hereafter.

Reverence, a Belief in God's Presence

"Thine eyes shall see the King in his beauty: they shall behold the land that is very far off." Isaiah 33:17.

Though Moses was not permitted to enter the land of promise, he was vouchsafed a sight of it from a distance. We too, though as yet we are not admitted to heavenly glory, yet are given to see much, in preparation for seeing more. Christ dwells among us in His Church really though invisibly, and through its Ordinances fulfils towards us, in a true and sufficient sense, the promise of the text. We are even now permitted to "see the King in His beauty," to "behold the land that is very far off." The words of the Prophet relate to our present state as well as to the state of saints hereafter. Of the future glory it is said by St. John, "They shall see His face, and His name shall be in their foreheads."[7] And of the present, Isaiah himself speaks in passages which may be taken in explanation of the text: "The glory of the Lord shall be revealed, and all flesh shall see it together;" and again, "They shall see the glory of the Lord, and the excellency of our God."[8] We do not see God face to face under the Gospel, but still, for all that, it is true that "we know in part;" we see, though it be "through a glass darkly;" which is far more than any but Christians are enabled to do. Baptism, by which we become Christians, is an illumination; and Christ, who

---

[7] Rev. 22:4
[8] Isa. 40:5; 35:2

is the Object of our worship, is withal a Light to worship by.

Such a view is strange to most men; they do not realize the presence of Christ, nor admit the duty of realizing it. Even those who are not without habits of seriousness, have almost or quite forgotten the duty. This is plain at once: for, unless they had, they would not be so very deficient in reverence as they are. It is scarcely too much to say that awe and fear are at the present day all but discarded from religion. Whole societies called Christian make it almost a first principle to disown the duty of reverence; and we ourselves, to whom as children of the Church reverence is as a special inheritance, have very little of it, and do not feel the want of it. Those who, in spite of themselves, are influenced by God's holy fear, too often are ashamed of it, consider it even as a mark of weakness of mind, hide their feeling as much as they can, and, when ridiculed or censured for it, cannot defend it to themselves on intelligible grounds. They wish indeed to maintain reverence in their mode of speaking and acting, in relation to sacred things, but they are at a loss how to answer objections, or how to resist received customs and fashions; and at length they begin to be suspicious and afraid of their own instinctive feelings. Let us then take occasion from the promise in the text both to describe the religious defect to which I have alluded, and to state the remedy for it.

There are two classes of men who are deficient in awe and fear, and, lamentable to say, taken together, they go far to make up the religious portion of the community. This is lamentable indeed, if so it is: it is not wonderful that sinners should live without the fear of God; but what shall we say of an age or country, in which even the more serious classes, those who live on principle, and claim to have a judgment in religious matters, who look forward to the future, and think that their account stands fair, and that they are in God's favour, when even such persons maintain, or at least act as if they maintained, that "the spirit of God's holy fear" is no part of religion? "If the light that is in us be darkness, how great is that darkness!"

These are the two classes of men who are deficient in this respect: first, those who think that they never were greatly under God's displeasure; next, those who think that, though they once were, they are not at all now for all sin has been forgiven them;—those on the one hand who consider that sin is no great evil in itself, those on the other who consider that it is no great evil in them, because their persons are accepted in Christ for their faith's sake.

Now it must be observed that the existence of fear in religion does not depend on the circumstance of our being sinners; it is short of that. Were we pure as the Angels, yet in His sight, one should think, we could not but fear, before whom the heavens are not clean, nor the Angels free from folly. The Seraphim themselves veiled their faces while they cried, Glory! Even then were it true that sin was not a great evil, or was no great evil in us, nevertheless the mere circumstance that God is infinite and all-perfect is an overwhelming thought to creatures and mortal men, and ought to lead all persons who profess religion to profess also religious fear, however natural it is for irreligious men to disclaim the feeling.

And next let it be observed, it is no dispute about terms. For at first sight we may be tempted to think that the only question is whether the word "fear" is a good or bad word—that one man makes it all one with slavish dread, and another with godly awe and reverence; and that therefore the two seem to oppose each other, when they do not, as if both parties agreed that reverence is right and selfish terror wrong, and the only point between them were, whether by the word fear was meant terror or reverence. This is not the case: it is a question not of words but of things; for these persons whom I am describing plainly consider that state of mind wrong, which the Church Catholic has ever prescribed and her Saints have ever exemplified.

To show that this is so, I will in a few words state what the two sets of opinion are to which I allude; and what that fault is, which, widely as they differ in opinion from each other, they have in common.

The one class of persons consists of those who think the Catholic Creed too strict—who hold that no certain doctrines need be believed in order to salvation, or at least question the necessity; who say that it matters not what a man believes, so that his conduct is respectable and orderly—who think that all rites and ceremonies are mere niceties (as they speak) and trifles, and that a man pleases God equally by observing them or not—who perhaps go on to doubt whether Christ's death is strictly speaking an atonement for the sin of man—who, when pressed, do not allow that He is strictly speaking and literally God—and who deny that the punishment of the wicked is eternal. Such are the tenets, more or less clearly apprehended and confessed, which mark the former of the two classes of which I speak.

The other class of men are in their formal doctrines widely different from the former. They consider that, though they were by nature children of wrath, they are now by God's grace so fully in His favour, that, were they to die at once, they would be certain of heaven— they consider that God so absolutely forgives them day by day their trespasses, that they have nothing to answer for, nothing to be tried upon at the Last Day—that they have been visited by God's grace in a manner quite distinct from all around them, and are His children in a sense in which others are not, and have an assurance of their saving state peculiar to themselves, and an interest in the promises such as Baptism does not impart—they profess to be thus beyond the reach of doubt and anxiety, and they say that they should be miserable without such a privilege.

I have alluded to these schools of religion, to show how widely a feeling must be spread which such contrary classes of men have in common. Now, what they agree in is this: in considering God as simply a God of love, not of awe and reverence also—the one meaning by love *benevolence*, and the other *mercy*; and in consequence neither the one nor the other regard Almighty God with *fear*; and the signs of want of fear in both the one and the other, which I proposed to point out, are such as the following.

For instance: they have no scruple or misgiving in speaking freely of Almighty God. They will use His Name as familiarly and lightly, as if they were open sinners. The one class adopts a set of words to denote Almighty God, which remove the idea of His personality, speaking of Him as the "Deity," or the "Divine Being;" which, as they use them, are of all others most calculated to remove from the mind the thought of a living and intelligent Governor, their Saviour and their Judge. The other class of men, going into the other extreme, but with the same result, use freely that incommunicable Name by which He has vouchsafed to denote to us His perfections. When He appeared to Moses, He disclosed His Name; and that Name has appeared so sacred to our translators of Scripture, that they have scrupled to use it, though it occurs continually in the Old Testament, substituting the word "Lord" out of reverence. Now, the persons in question delight in a familiar use, in prayers and hymns and conversation, of that Name by which they designate Him before whom Angels tremble. Not even our fellow-men do we freely call by their own names, unless we are at our ease with them; yet sinners can bear to be familiar with the Name by which they know the Most High has distinguished Himself from all creatures.

Another instance of want of fear, is the bold and unscrupulous way in which men speak of the Holy Trinity and the Mystery of the Divine Nature. They use sacred terms and phrases, should occasion occur, in a rude and abrupt way, and discuss points of doctrine concerning the All-holy and Eternal, even (if I may without irreverence state it) over their cups, perhaps arguing against them, as if He were such a one as themselves.

Another instance of this want of fear is found in the peremptory manner in which men lay down what Almighty God must do, what He cannot but do, as if they were masters of the whole scheme of salvation, and might anticipate His high providence and will.

And another is the confidence with which they often speak of their having been converted, pardoned, and sanctified, as if they knew their own state as well as God knows it.

Another is the unwillingness so commonly felt, to bow at the Name of Jesus, nay the impatience exhibited towards those who do; as if there were nothing awful in the idea of the Eternal God being made man, and as if we did not suitably express our wonder and awe at it by practising what St. Paul has in very word prescribed.

Another instance is the careless mode in which men speak of our Lord's earthly doings and sayings, just as if He were a mere man. He was man indeed, but He was more than man: and He did what man does, but then those deeds of His were the deeds of God—and we can as little separate the deed from the Doer as our arm from our body. But, in spite of this, numbers are apt to use rude, familiar, profane language, concerning their God's childhood, and youth, and ministry, though He is their God.

And another is the familiarity with which many persons address our Lord in prayer, applying epithets to Him and adopting a strain of language which does not beseem creatures, not to say sinners.

And another is their general mode of prayer; I mean, in diffuse and free language, with emphatic and striking words, in a sort of coloured or rich style, with pomp of manner, and an oratorical tone, as if praying were preaching, and as if its object were not to address Almighty God, but to impress and affect those who heard them.

And another instance of this want of reverence is the introduction, in speaking or writing, of serious and solemn words, for the sake of effect, to round, or to give dignity to, a sentence.

And another instance is irreverence in church, sitting instead of kneeling in prayer, or pretending to kneel but really sitting, or lounging or indulging in other unseemly attitudes; and, much more, looking about when prayers are going on, and observing what others are doing.

These are some out of a number of peculiarities which mark the religion of the day, and are instanced some in one class of men, some in another; but all by one or other;—and they are specimens of what I mean when I say that the religion of this day is destitute of *fear*.

Many other instances might be mentioned of very various kinds. For instance, the freedom with which men propose to alter God's ordinances, to suit their own convenience, or to meet the age; their reliance on their private and antecedent notions about sacred subjects; their want of interest and caution in inquiring what God's probable will is; their contempt for any view of the Sacraments which exceeds the evidence of their senses; and their confidence in settling the order of importance in which the distinct articles of Christian faith stand;—all which shows that it is no question of words whether men have fear or not, but that there is a something they really have not, whatever name we give it.

So far I consider to be plain: the only point which can be debated is this, whether the feelings which I have been describing are necessary; for each of the two classes which I have named contends that they are unnecessary; the one decides them inconsistent with reason, the other with the Gospel; the one calls them superstitious, and the other legal or Jewish. Let us then consider, are these feelings of fear and awe Christian feelings or not? A very few words will surely be sufficient to decide the question.

I say this, then, which I think no one can reasonably dispute. They are the class of feelings we *should* have—yes, have in an intense degree—if we literally had the sight of Almighty God; therefore they are the class of feelings which we shall have, *if* we realize His presence. In proportion as we believe that He is present, we shall have them; and not to have them, is not to realize, not to believe that He is present. If then it is a duty to feel as though we saw Him, or to have faith, it is a duty to have these feelings; and if it is a sin to be destitute of faith, it is a sin to be without them. Let us consider this awhile.

Who then is there to deny, that if we saw God, we should fear? Take the most cold and secular of all those who explain away the Gospel; or take the most heated and fanatic of those who consider it peculiarly their own; take those who think that Christ has brought us nothing great, or those who think He has brought it all to themselves—I say, would either party keep from fearing greatly if they saw God? Surely it is quite a truism to say that any creature would fear. But why would he fear? would it be merely because he saw God, or because he knew that God was present? If he shut his eyes, he would still fear, for his eyes had conveyed to him this solemn truth; to *have* seen would be enough. But if so, does it not follow at once, that, if men do not fear, it is because they do not act as they would act if they saw Him, that is—they do not feel that He is present? Is it not quite certain that men would not use Almighty God's Name so freely, if they thought He was really in hearing,—nay, close beside them when they spoke? And so of those other instances of want of godly fear, which I mentioned, they one and all come from deadness to the presence of God. If a man believes Him present, he will shrink from addressing Him familiarly, or using before Him unreal words, or peremptorily and on his own judgment deciding what God's will is, or claiming His confidence, or addressing Him in a familiar posture of body. I say, take the man who is most confident that he has nothing to fear from the presence of God, and that Almighty God is at peace with him, and place him actually before the throne of God; and would he have no misgivings? and will he dare to say that those misgivings are a weakness, a mere irrational perturbation, which he ought not to feel?

This will be seen more clearly, by considering how differently we feel towards and speak of our friends as present or absent. Their presence is a check upon us; it acts as an external law, compelling us to do or not do what we should not do or do otherwise, or should do but for it. This is just what most men lack in their religion at present—such an external restraint arising from the consciousness of God's presence. Consider, I say, how differently we speak of a friend, however intimate, when present or absent; consider how we feel, should it so happen that we have begun to speak of him as if he were not present, on finding suddenly that he is; and that, though we are conscious of nothing but what is loving and open towards him. There is a tone of voice and a manner of speaking about persons absent, which we should consider disrespectful, or at least inconsiderate, if they were present. When that is the case, we are ever thinking more or less, even though unconsciously to ourselves, how they will take what we say, how it will affect them, what they will say to us or think of us in turn. When a person is absent, we are tempted perhaps confidently to say what his opinion is on certain points; but should he be present, we qualify our words; we hardly like to speak at all, from the vivid consciousness that we may be wrong, and that he is present to tell us so. We are very cautious of pronouncing what his feelings are on the matter in hand, or how he is disposed towards ourselves; and in all things we observe a deference and delicacy in our conduct towards him. Now, if we feel this towards our fellows, what shall we feel in the presence of an Angel? and if so, what in the presence of the All-knowing, All-searching Judge of men? What is respect and consideration in the case of our fellows, becomes godly fear as regards Almighty God; and they who do not fear Him, in one word, do not believe that He sees and hears them. If they did, they would cease to boast so confidently of His favourable thoughts of them, to foretell His dealings, to pronounce upon His revelations, to make free with His Name, and to address Him familiarly.

Now, in what has been said, no account has been taken, as I have already observed, of our being sinners, a corrupt, polluted race at the best, while He is the All-holy God—which must surely increase our fear and awe greatly, and not at all the less because we have been so wonderfully redeemed. Nor, again, has account been taken of another point, on which I will add two or three words.

There is a peculiar feeling with which we regard the dead. What does this arise from?—that he is absent? No; for we do not feel the same towards one who is merely distant, though he be at the other end of the earth. Is it because in this life we shall never see him again? No, surely not; because we may be perfectly certain we shall never see him when he goes abroad, we may know he is to die abroad, and perhaps he does die abroad; but will any one say that, when the news of his death comes, our feeling when we think of him is not quite changed? Surely it is the passing into another state which impresses itself upon us, and makes us speak of him as we do,—I mean, with a sort of awe. We cannot tell what he is now,—what his relations to us,—what he knows of us. We do not understand him,—we do not see him. He is passed into the land "that is very far off;" but it is not at all certain that he has not some mysterious hold over us. Thus his not being seen with our bodily eyes, while perchance he is present, makes the thought of him more awful. Apply this to the subject before us, and you will perceive that there is a sense, and a true sense, in which the *invisible* presence of God is more awful and overpowering than if we saw it. And so again, the presence of Christ, now that it is invisible, brings with it a host of high and mysterious feelings, such as nothing else can inspire. The thought of our Saviour, absent yet present, is like that of a friend taken from us, but, as it were, in dream returned to us, though in this case not in dream, but in reality and truth. When He was going away, He said to His disciples, "I will see you again, and your heart shall rejoice." Yet He had at another time said, "The days will come when the Bridegroom shall be taken from them, and then shall they fast in those days." See what an apparent contradiction, such as attends the putting any high feeling into human language! they were to joy because Christ was come, and yet weep because He was away; that is, to have a feeling so refined, so strange and new, that nothing could be said of it, but that it combined in one all that was sweet and soothing in contrary human feelings, as commonly experienced. As some precious fruits of the earth are said to taste like all others at once, not as not being really distinct from all others, but as being thus best described, when we would come as near the truth as we can, so the state of mind which they are in who believe that the Son of God is here, yet away,—is at the right hand of God, yet in His very flesh and blood among us,—is present, though invisible,—is one of both joy and pain, or rather one far above either; a feeling of awe, wonder, and praise, which cannot be more suitably expressed than by the Scripture word *fear*; or by holy Job's words, though he spoke in grief, and not as being possessed of a blessing. "Behold, I go forward, but He is not there; and backward, but I cannot perceive Him: on the left hand, where He doth work, but I cannot behold Him: He hideth Himself on the right hand, that I cannot see Him. Therefore am I troubled at His presence; when I consider, I am afraid of Him."[9]

To conclude. Enough has been said now to show that godly fear must be a duty, if to live as in God's presence is a duty—must be a privilege of the Gospel, if the spiritual sight of "the King in His beauty" be one of its privileges. Fear follows from faith necessarily, as would be plain, even though there were not a text in the Bible saying so. But in fact, as it is scarcely needful to say, Scripture abounds in precepts to fear God. Such are the words of the Wise Man: "The fear of the Lord is the beginning of knowledge." Such again is the third commandment, in which we are solemnly bidden not to take God's Name in vain. Such the declaration of the prophet Habakkuk, who beginning by declaring "The

---

[9] Job 23:8, 9, 15

just shall live by his faith," ends by saying, "The Lord is in His Holy Temple; let the whole earth keep silence before Him." Such is St. Paul's, who, in like manner, after having discoursed at length upon faith as "the realizing of things hoped for, the evidence of things not seen," adds: "Let us have grace, whereby we may serve God acceptably with reverence and godly fear." Such St. Luke's account of the Church militant on earth, that "walking in the fear of the Lord and in the comfort of the Holy Ghost," it was "multiplied." Such St. John's account of the Church triumphant in heaven, "Who shall not fear Thee," they say, "O Lord, and glorify Thy Name; for Thou only art Holy?" Such the feeling recorded of the three Apostles on the Mount of Transfiguration, who, when they heard God's voice, "fell on their face, and were sore afraid."[10] And now, if this be so, can anything be clearer than that the *want* of fear is nothing else but *want* of faith, and that in consequence we in this age are approaching in religious temper that evil day of which it is said, "When the Son of Man cometh, shall He find faith on the earth?"[11] Is it wonderful that we have no fear in our words and mutual intercourse, when we exercise no *acts* of faith? What, you will ask, are acts of faith? Such as these,—to come often to prayer, is an act of faith; to kneel down instead of sitting, is an act of faith; to strive to attend to your prayers, is an act of faith; to behave in God's House otherwise than you would in a common room, is an act of faith; to come to it on weekdays as well as

---

[10] Prov. 1:7; Hab. 2:4, 20; Heb. 12:28; Acts 9:31; Rev. 25:4; Matt. 17:6

[11] Luke 18:8

Sundays, is an act of faith; to come often to the most Holy Sacrament, is an act of faith; and to be still and reverent during that sacred service, is an act of faith. These are all acts of faith, because they all are acts such as we should perform, if we saw and heard Him who *is* present, though with our bodily eyes we see and hear Him *not*. But, "blessed are they who have not seen, and yet have believed;" for, be sure, if we thus act, we shall, through God's grace, be gradually endued with the spirit of His holy fear. We shall in time, in our mode of talking and acting, in our religious services and our daily conduct, manifest, not with constraint and effort, but spontaneously and naturally, that we fear Him while we love him.

Unreal Words

"Thine eyes shall see the King in His beauty: they shall behold the land that is very far off." Isaiah 33:17.

The Prophet tells us, that under the Gospel covenant God's servants will have the privilege of seeing those heavenly sights which were but shadowed out in the Law. Before Christ came was the time of shadows; but when He came, He brought truth as well as grace; and as He who is the Truth has come to us, so does He in return require that we should be true and sincere in our dealings with Him. To be true and sincere is really to see with our minds those great wonders which He has wrought in order that we might see them. When God opened the eyes of the ass on which Balaam rode, she saw the Angel and acted upon the sight. When He opened the eyes of the young man, Elisha's servant, he too saw the chariots and horses of fire, and took comfort. And in like manner, Christians are now under the protection of a Divine Presence, and that more wonderful than any which was vouchsafed of old time. God revealed Himself visibly to Jacob, to Job, to Moses, to Joshua, and to Isaiah; to us He reveals Himself not visibly, but more wonderfully and truly; not without the cooperation of our own will, but upon our faith, and for that very reason more truly; for faith is the special means of gaining spiritual blessings. Hence St. Paul prays for the Ephesians "that Christ may dwell in their hearts by faith," and that "the eyes of their understanding may be enlightened." And St. John declares that "the Son of God hath given us an understanding that we may know Him that is true: and we are in Him that is true, even in His Son Jesus Christ."[12]

We are no longer then in the region of shadows: we have the true Saviour set before us, the true reward, and the true means of spiritual renewal. We know the true state of the soul by nature and by grace, the evil of sin, the consequences of sinning, the way of pleasing God, and the motives to act upon. God has revealed Himself clearly to us; He has "destroyed the face of the covering cast over all people, and the veil that is spread over all nations." "The darkness is past, and the True Light now shineth."[13] And therefore, I say, He calls upon us in turn to "walk in the light as He is in the light." The Pharisees might have this excuse in their hypocrisy, that the plain truth had not been revealed to them; we have not even this poor reason for insincerity. We have no opportunity of mistaking one thing for another: the promise is expressly made to us that "our teachers shall not be removed into a corner any more, but our eyes shall see our teachers;" that "the eyes of them that see shall not be dim;" that every thing shall be called by its right name; that "the vile person shall be no more called liberal, nor the churl said to be bountiful;"[14] in a word, as the text speaks, that "our eyes shall see the king in His beauty; we shall behold the land that is very far off." Our professions, our creeds, our prayers, our dealings, our conversation, our arguments, our teaching must henceforth be sincere, or,

---

12 Ephes. 3:17; 1:18; 1 John 5:20
13 Isa. 25:7; 1 John 2:8
14 Isa. 30:20; 32:3, 5

to use an expressive word, must be *real*. What St. Paul says of himself and his fellow-laborers, that they were true because Christ is true, applies to all Christians: "Our rejoicing is this, the testimony of our conscience, that in simplicity and godly sincerity, not with fleshly wisdom, but by the grace of God, we have had our conversation in the world, and more abundantly to you-ward... The things that I purpose, do I purpose according to the flesh, that with me there should be yea yea, and nay nay? But as God is true, our word toward you was not yea and nay. For the Son of God, Jesus Christ... was not yea and nay, but in Him was yea. For all the promises of God in Him are yea, and in Him Amen, unto the glory of God by us." [15]

And yet it need scarcely be said, nothing is so rare as honesty and singleness of mind; so much so, that a person who is really honest, is already perfect. Insincerity was an evil which sprang up within the Church from the first; Ananias and Simon were not open opposers of the Apostles, but false brethren. And, as foreseeing what was to be, our Saviour is remarkable in His ministry for nothing more than the earnestness of the dissuasives which He addressed to those who came to Him, against taking up religion lightly, or making promises which they were likely to break.

Thus He, "the True Light, which lighteth every man that cometh into the world," "the Amen, the faithful and true Witness, the Beginning of the creation of God," [16] said to the young Ruler, who lightly called Him

---

[15] 2 Cor. 1:12-20
[16] John 1:9; Rev. 3:14

"Good Master," "Why callest thou Me good?" as bidding him weigh his words; and then abruptly told him, "One thing thou lackest." When a certain man professed that he would follow Him whithersoever He went, He did not respond to him, but said, "The foxes have holes, and the birds of the air have nests, but the Son of Man hath not where to lay His head." When St. Peter said with all his heart in the name of himself and brethren, "To whom shall we go? Thou hast the words of eternal life," He answered pointedly, "Have not I chosen you twelve, and one of you is a devil?" as if He said, "Answer for thyself." When the two Apostles professed their desire to cast their lot with Him, He asked whether they could "drink of His cup, and be baptized with His baptism." And when "there went great multitudes with Him," He turned and said, that unless a man hated relations, friends, and self, he could not be His disciple. And then he proceeded to warn all men to "count the cost" ere they followed Him. Such is the merciful severity with which He repels us that He may gain us more truly. And what He thinks of those who, after coming to Him, relapse into a hollow and hypocritical profession, we learn from His language towards the Laodiceans: "I know thy works, that thou art neither cold nor hot: I would thou wert cold or hot. So then, because thou art lukewarm, and neither cold nor hot, I will cast thee out of My mouth."[17]

We have a striking instance of the same conduct on the part of that ancient Saint who prefigured our Lord

---

[17] Mark 10:17-21; Matt. 8:20; John 6:68-70; Matt. 20:22; Luke 14:25-28; Rev. 3:15-16

in name and office, Joshua, the captain of the chosen people in entering Canaan. When they had at length taken possession of that land which Moses and their fathers had seen "very far off," they said to him, "God forbid that we should forsake the Lord, and serve other gods. We will…serve the Lord, for He is our God." He made answer, "Ye cannot serve the Lord; for He is a holy God; He is a jealous God; He will not forgive your transgressions nor your sins."[18] Not as if he would hinder them from obeying, but to sober them in professing. How does his answer remind us of St Paul's still more awful words, about the impossibility of renewal after utterly falling away!

And what is said of profession of *discipleship* applies undoubtedly in its degree to *all* profession. To make professions is to play with edged tools, unless we attend to what we are saying. Words have a meaning, whether we mean that meaning or not; and they are imputed to us in their real meaning, when our not meaning it is our own fault. He who takes God's Name in vain, is not counted guiltless because he means nothing by it,—he cannot frame a language for himself; and they who make professions, of whatever kind, are heard in the sense of those professions, and are not excused because they themselves attach no sense to them. "By thy words thou shalt be justified, and by thy words thou shalt be condemned."[19]

Now this consideration needs especially to be pressed upon Christians at this day; for this is especially

---

[18] Josh. 24:16-19
[19] Matt. 12:37

a day of professions. You will answer in my own words, that all ages have been ages of profession. So they have been, in one way or other, but this day in its own especial sense;—because this is especially a day of individual profession. This is a day in which there is (rightly or wrongly) so much of private judgment, so much of separation and difference, so much of preaching and teaching, so much of authorship, that it involves individual profession, responsibility, and recompense in a way peculiarly its own. It will not then be out of place if, in connexion with the text, we consider some of the many ways in which persons, whether in this age or in another, make unreal professions, or seeing see not, and hearing hear not, and speak without mastering, or trying to master, their words. This I will attempt to do at some length, and in matters of detail, which are not the less important because they are minute.

Of course it is very common in all matters, not only in religion, to speak in an unreal way; viz., when we speak on a subject with which our minds are not familiar. If you were to hear a person who knew nothing about military matters, giving directions how soldiers on service should conduct themselves, or how their food and lodging, or their marching, was to be duly arranged, you would be sure that his mistakes would be such as to excite the ridicule and contempt of men experienced in warfare. If a foreigner were to come to one of our cities, and without hesitation offer plans for the supply of our markets, or the management of our police, it is so certain that he would expose himself, that the very attempt would argue a great want of good sense and modesty. We should feel that he did not understand us, and that when he spoke about us, he would be using words without meaning. If a dim-sighted man were to attempt to decide questions of proportion and colour, or a man without ear to judge of musical compositions, we should feel that he spoke on and from general principles, on fancy, or by deduction and argument, not from a real apprehension of the matters which he discussed. His remarks would be theoretical and unreal.

This unsubstantial way of speaking is instanced in the case of persons who fall into any new company among strange faces and amid novel occurrences. They sometimes form amiable judgments of men and things, sometimes the reverse,—but whatever their judgments be, they are to those who know the men and the things strangely unreal and distorted. They feel reverence where they should not; they discern slights where none were intended; they discover meaning in events which have none; they fancy motives; they misinterpret manner; they mistake character; and they form generalizations and combinations which exist only in their own minds.

Again, persons who have not attended to the subject of morals, or to politics, or to matters ecclesiastical, or to theology, do not know the relative value of questions which they meet with in these departments of knowledge. They do not understand the difference between one point and another. The one and the other are the same to them. They look at them as infants gaze at the objects which meet their eyes, in a vague unapprehensive way, as if not knowing whether a thing is a hundred miles off or close at hand, whether great or small, hard or soft. They have no means of judging, no standard to measure by,—and they give judgment at random, saying yea or nay on very deep questions, according as their fancy is struck at the moment, or as some clever or specious argument happens to come across them. Consequently they are inconsistent; say one thing one day, another the next;—and if they must act, act in the dark; or if they can help acting, do not act; or if they act freely, act from some other reason not avowed. All this is to be unreal.

Again, there cannot be a more apposite specimen of unreality than the way in which judgments are commonly formed upon important questions by the mass of the community. Opinions are continually given in the world on matters, about which those who offer them are as little qualified to judge as blind men about colours, and that because they have never exercised their minds upon the points in question. This is a day in which all men are obliged to have an opinion on all questions, political, social, and religious, because they have in some way or other an influence upon the decision; yet the multitude are for the most part absolutely without capacity to take their part in it. In saying this, I am far from meaning that this need be so, —I am far from denying that there is such a thing as plain good sense, or (what is better) religious sense, which will see its way through very intricate matters, or that this is in fact sometimes exerted in the community at large on certain great questions; but at the same time this practical sense is so far from existing as regards the vast mass of questions which in this day come before the public, that (as all persons who attempt to gain the influence of the people on their side know well) their opinions must be purchased by interesting their prejudices or fears in their favour;—not by presenting a question in its real and true substance, but by adroitly colouring it, or selecting out of it some particular point which may be exaggerated, and dressed up, and be made the means of working on popular feelings. And thus government and the art of government becomes, as much as popular religion, hollow and unsound.

And hence it is that the popular voice is so changeable. One man or measure is the idol of the people today, another tomorrow. They have never got beyond accepting shadows for things.

What is instanced in the mass is instanced also in various ways in individuals, and in points of detail. For instance, some men are set perhaps on being eloquent speakers. They use great words and imitate the sentences of others; and they fancy that those whom they imitate had as little meaning as themselves, or they perhaps contrive to think that they themselves have a meaning adequate to their words.

Another sort of unreality, or voluntary profession of what is above us, is instanced in the conduct of those who suddenly come into power or place. They affect a manner such as they think the office requires, but which is beyond them, and therefore unbecoming. They wish to act with dignity, and they cease to be themselves.

And so again, to take a different case, many men, when they come near persons in distress and wish to show sympathy, often condole in a very unreal way. I am not altogether laying this to their fault; for it is very difficult to know what to do, when on the one hand we cannot realize to ourselves the sorrow, yet withal wish to be kind to those who feel it. A tone of grief seems necessary, yet (if so be) cannot under our circumstances be genuine. Yet even here surely there is a true way, if we could find it, by which pretence may be avoided, and yet respect and consideration shown.

And in like manner as regards religious emotions. Persons are aware from the mere force of the doctrines of which the Gospel consists, that they ought to be variously affected, and deeply and intensely too, in consequence of them. The doctrines of original and actual sin, of Christ's Divinity and Atonement, and of Holy Baptism, are so vast, that no one can realize them without very complicated and profound feelings. Natural reason tells a man this, and that if he simply and genuinely believes the doctrines, he must have these feelings; and he professes to believe the doctrines absolutely, and therefore he professes the correspondent feelings. But in truth he perhaps does *not* really believe them absolutely, because such absolute belief is the work of long time, and therefore his profession of feeling outruns the real inward existence of feeling, or he becomes unreal. Let us never lose sight of two truths,—that we ought to have our hearts penetrated with the love of Christ and full of self-renunciation; but that if they be not, professing that they are does not make them so.

Again, to take a more serious instance of the same fault, some persons pray, not as sinners addressing their God, not as the Publican smiting on his breast, and saying, "God be merciful to me a sinner," but in such a way as they conceive to be becoming *under* circumstances of guilt, in a way becoming such a strait. They are self-conscious, and reflect on what they are about, and instead of actually approaching (as it were) the mercy-seat, they are filled with the thought that God is great, and man His creature, God on high and man on earth, and that they are engaged in a high and solemn service, and that they ought to rise up to its sublime and momentous character.

Another still more common form of the same fault, yet without any definite pretence or effort, is the mode in which people speak of the shortness and vanity of life, the certainty of death, and the joys of heaven. They have commonplaces in their mouths, which they bring forth upon occasions for the good of others, or to console them, or as a proper and becoming mark of attention towards them. Thus they speak to clergymen in a professedly serious way, making remarks true and sound, and in themselves deep, yet unmeaning in their mouths; or they give advice to children or young men; or perhaps in low spirits or sickness they are led to speak in a religious strain as if it was spontaneous. Or when they fall into sin, they speak of man being frail, of the deceitfulness of the human heart, of God's mercy, and so on—all these great words, heaven, hell, judgment, mercy, repentance, works, the world that now is, the world to come, being little more than "lifeless sounds, whether of pipe or harp," in their mouths and ears, as the "very lovely song of one that hath a pleasant voice and can play well on an instrument"—as the proprieties of conversation, or the civilities of good breeding.

I am speaking of the conduct of the world at large, called Christian; but what has been said applies, and necessarily, to the case of a number of well-disposed or even religious men. I mean, that before men come to know the realities of human life, it is not wonderful that their view of religion should be unreal. Young people who have never known sorrow or anxiety, or the sacrifices which conscientiousness involves, want commonly that depth and seriousness of character, which sorrow only and anxiety and self-sacrifice can give. I do not notice this as a fault, but as a plain fact, which may often be seen, and which it is well to bear in mind. This is the legitimate use of this world, to make us seek for another. It does its part when it repels us and disgusts us and drives us elsewhere. Experience of it gives experience of that which is its antidote, in the case of religious minds; and we become real in our view of what is spiritual by the contact of things temporal and earthly. And much more are men unreal when they have some secret motive urging them a different way from religion, and when their professions therefore are forced into an unnatural course in order to subserve their secret motive. When men do not like the conclusions to which their principles lead, or the precepts which Scripture contains, they are not wanting in ingenuity to blunt their force. They can frame some theory, or dress up certain objections, to defend themselves withal; a theory, that is, or objections, which it is difficult to refute perhaps, but which any rightly-ordered mind, nay, any common bystander, perceives to be unnatural and insincere.

What has been here noticed of individuals, takes place even in the case of whole Churches, at times when love has waxed cold and faith failed. The whole system of the Church, its discipline and ritual, are all in their origin the spontaneous and exuberant fruit of the real principle of spiritual religion in the hearts of its members. The invisible Church has developed itself into the Church visible, and its outward rites and forms are nourished and animated by the living power which dwells within it. Thus every part of it is real, down to the minutest details. But when the seductions of the world and the lusts of the flesh have eaten out this divine inward life, what is the outward Church but a hollowness and a mockery, like the whited sepulchres of which our Lord speaks, a memorial of what was and is not? and though we trust that the Church is nowhere thus utterly deserted by the Spirit of truth, at least according to God's ordinary providence, yet may we not say that in proportion as it approaches to this state of deadness, the grace of its ordinances, though not forfeited, at least flows in but a scanty or uncertain stream?

And lastly, if this unreality may steal over the Church itself, which is in its very essence a practical institution, much more is it found in the philosophies and literature of men. Literature is almost in its essence unreal; for it is the exhibition of thought disjoined from practice. Its very home is supposed to be ease and retirement; and when it does more than speak or write, it is accused of transgressing its bounds. This indeed constitutes what is considered its true dignity and honour, viz. its abstraction from the actual affairs of life; its security from the world's currents and vicissitudes; its saying without doing. A man of literature is considered to preserve his dignity by doing nothing; and when he proceeds forward into action, he is thought to lose his position, as if he were degrading his calling by enthusiasm, and becoming a politician or a partisan. Hence mere literary men are able to say strong things against the opinions of their age, whether religious or political, without offence; because no one thinks they mean anything by them. They are not expected to go forward to act upon them, and mere words hurt no one.

Such are some of the more common or more extended specimens of profession without action, or of speaking without really seeing and feeling. In instancing which, let it be observed, I do not mean to say that such profession, as has been described, is always culpable and wrong; indeed I have implied the contrary throughout. It is often a misfortune. It takes a long time really to feel and understand things as they are; we learn to do so only gradually. Profession beyond our feelings is only a fault when we might help it;—when either we speak when we need not speak, or do not feel when we might have felt. Hard insensible hearts, ready and thoughtless talkers, these are they whose unreality, as I have termed it, is a sin; it is the sin of every one of us, in proportion as our hearts are cold, or our tongues excessive.

But the mere fact of our saying more than we feel is not necessarily sinful. St. Peter did not rise up to the full meaning of his confession, "Thou art the Christ," yet he was pronounced blessed. St. James and St. John said, "We are able," without clear apprehension, yet without offence. We ever promise things greater than we master, and we wait on God to enable us to perform them. Our promising involves a prayer for light and strength. And so again we all say the Creed, but who comprehends it fully? All we can hope is, that we are in the way to understand it; that we partly understand it; that we desire, pray, and strive to understand it more and more. Our Creed becomes a sort of prayer. Persons are culpably unreal in their way of speaking, not when they say more than they feel, but when they say things different from what they feel. A miser praising almsgiving, or a coward giving rules for courage, is unreal; but it is not unreal for the less to discourse about the greater, for the liberal to descant upon munificence, or the generous to praise the noble-minded, or the self-denying to use the language of the austere, or the confessor to exhort to martyrdom.

What I have been saying comes to this: be in earnest, and you will speak of religion where, and when, and how you should; aim at things, and your words will be right without aiming. There are ten thousand ways of looking at this world, but only one right way. The man of pleasure has his way, the man of gain his, and the man of intellect his. Poor men and rich men, governors and governed, prosperous and discontented, learned and unlearned, each has his own way of looking at the things which come before him, and each has a wrong way. There is but one right way; it is the way in which God looks at the world. Aim at looking at it in God's way. Aim at seeing things as God sees them. Aim at forming judgments about persons, events, ranks, fortunes, changes, objects, such as God forms. Aim at looking at this life as God looks at it. Aim at looking at the life to come, and the world unseen, as God does. Aim at "seeing the King in his beauty." All things that we see are but shadows to us and delusions, unless we enter into what they really mean.

It is not an easy thing to learn that new language which Christ has brought us. He has interpreted all things for us in a new way; He has brought us a religion which sheds a new light on all that happens. Try to learn this language. Do not get it by rote, or speak it as a thing of course. Try to understand what you say. Time is short, eternity is long; God is great, man is weak; he stands between heaven and hell; Christ is his Saviour; Christ has suffered for him. The Holy Ghost sanctifies him; repentance purifies him, faith justifies, works save. These are solemn truths, which need not be actually spoken, except in the way of creed or of teaching; but which must be laid up in the heart. That a thing is true, is no reason that it should be said, but that it should be done; that it should be acted upon; that it should be made our own inwardly.

Let us avoid talking, of whatever kind; whether mere empty talking, or censorious talking, or idle profession, or descanting upon Gospel doctrines, or the affectation of philosophy, or the pretence of eloquence. Let us guard against frivolity, love of display, love of being talked about, love of singularity, love of seeming original. Let us aim at meaning what we say, and saying what we mean; let us aim at knowing when we understand a truth, and when we do not. When we do not, let us take it on faith, and let us profess to do so. Let us receive the truth in reverence, and pray God to give us a good will, and divine light, and spiritual strength, that it may bear fruit within us.

Shrinking from Christ's Coming

"Thine eyes shall see the King in His beauty: they shall behold the land that is very far off." Isaiah 33:17.

Before Christ came, the faithful remnant of Israel were consoled with the promise that "their eyes should see" Him, who was to be their "salvation." "Unto you that fear My Name shall the Sun of righteousness arise with healing in His wings." Yet it is observable that the prophecy, though cheering and encouraging, had with it something of an awful character too. First, it was said, "The Lord whom ye seek shall suddenly come to His Temple, even the messenger of the Covenant whom ye delight in." Yet it is soon added, "But who may abide the day of His coming? and who shall stand when He appeareth? for He is like a refiner's fire, and like fullers' soap."[20]

The same mixture of fear with comfort is found in the Disciples after His Resurrection. The women departed from the sepulchre "with fear and great joy." They "trembled and were amazed: neither said they any thing to any man, for they were afraid." The Apostles "were terrified and affrighted, and supposed that they had seen a spirit." "They believed not for joy, and wondered." And our Lord said to them, "Why are ye troubled? and why do thoughts arise in your hearts?" On another occasion, "None of the disciples durst ask him, Who art thou? knowing that it was the Lord."[21] It

---

[20] Mal. 4:2; 3:1-2
[21] Matt. 28:8; Mark 16:8; Luke 24:37-38; John 21:12

might be from slowness to believe, or from misconception, or from the mere perplexity of amazement, but so it was; they exulted and they were awed.

Still more remarkable is the account of our Lord's appearance to St. John in the Book of Revelation; more remarkable because St. John had no doubt or perplexity. Christ had ascended; the Apostle had received the gift of the Holy Ghost; yet he "fell at His feet as dead."

This reflection leads us on to a parallel thought concerning the state and prospects of all Christians in every age. We too are looking out for Christ's coming, —we are bid look out,—we are bid pray for it; and yet it is to be a time of judgment. It is to be the deliverance of all Saints from sin and sorrow for ever; yet they, every one of them, must undergo an awful trial. How then can any look forward to it with joy, not knowing (for no one knows) the certainty of his own salvation? And the difficulty is increased when we come to pray for it—to pray for its coming soon: how can we pray that Christ would come, that the day of judgment would hasten, that His kingdom would come, that His kingdom may be at once—may come on us this day or tomorrow—when by so coming He would be shortening the time of our present life, and cut off those precious years given us for conversion, amendment, repentance and sanctification? Is there not an inconsistency in professing to wish our Judge already come, when we do not feel ourselves ready for Him? In what sense can we really and heartily pray that He would cut short the time, when our conscience tells us that, even were our life longest, we should have much to do in a few years?

I do not deny that there is some difficulty in the question, but surely not more so than there is on every side of us in religious matters. Religion has (as it were) its very life in what are paradoxes and contradictions in the eye of reason. It is a seeming inconsistency how we can pray for Christ's coming, yet wish time to "work out our salvation," and "make our calling and election sure." It was a seeming contradiction, how good men were to desire His first coming, yet be unable to abide it; how the Apostles feared, yet rejoiced after His resurrection. And so it is a paradox how the Christian should in all things be sorrowful yet always rejoicing, and dying yet living, and having nothing yet possessing all things. Such seeming contradictions arise from the want of depth in our minds to master the whole truth. We have not eyes keen enough to follow out the lines of God's providence and will, which meet at length, though at first sight they seem parallel.

I will now try to explain how these opposite duties of fearing yet praying to have the sight of Christ are not necessarily inconsistent with each other. Why we should fear it, is not strange. Surely when a man gets himself steadily to contemplate a state of things beyond this life, he is in the way to be overpowered by the thoughts which throng upon him. How dreadful to the imagination is every scene of that unknown hereafter! This life indeed is full of dangers and pains, but we know what they are like; we do not know what shall be in the world to come. "Lord, whither goest

Thou?" said the Apostles; "we know not whither Thou goest." Supposing a man told that he should suddenly be carried off to some unknown globe in the heavens, —this is the kind of trouble in its least fearful shape, which the future presents, when dwelt upon. And still more trying is the peculiar prospect which presents itself of Christ's coming in judgment. What a prospect, to be judged for all our doings by an unerring Judge. Try to trace back the history of your life in memory, and fancy every part of it confessed by you in words, put into words before some intimate friend, how great would be your shame! but how gladly would you in that day resign yourself to a disclosure to a fellow-sinner, how gladly to a disclosure to a world of sinners, compared with the presence of an All-holy, All-seeing Creator with His eyes upon you, "beholding you," as the gospel speaks of Him in the days of His flesh,— and one deed of evil after another told forth, while all your best actions and best qualities fade away and become as discoloured and unsightly as if there were nothing good in them; and you the while uncertain how the decision shall be. I do not presume to say that all this will happen in detail; but this is what is meant by a judgment in the earthly sense of the word, and that awful trial is surely not called a judgment for nothing, but that we may gain some ideas from it. Think of all this, and you will not deny that the thought of standing before Christ is enough to make us tremble. And yet His presence is held out to us by Himself as the greatest of goods; all Christians are bound to pray for it, to pray for its hastening; to pray that we may speedily look on Him whom none can see "without holiness," none but "the pure in heart;"—and now the question is, How can we pray for it with sincerity?

1. Now first, though we could not at all reconcile our feelings about ourselves with the command given us, still it is our duty to obey the latter on faith. If Abraham could lift up his knife to slay his son, we may well so far subdue our fears as to pray for what nevertheless is terrible. Job said, "Though he slay me, yet I will trust in him." Under all circumstances surely, we may calmly resign ourselves into His hands. Can we suppose that He would deceive us? deal unkindly or hardly with us? Can He make use of us, if I may say so, against ourselves? Let us not so think of the most merciful Lord. Let us do what He bids, and leave the rest to Him. Thus, I say, we might reason with ourselves, if nothing else could be said.

2. But next, I observe, that when we pray for the coming of Christ, we do but pray in the Church's words, that He would "*accomplish the number* of his elect and would hasten His kingdom." That is, we do not pray that He would simply cut short the world, but, so to express myself, that He would make time go quicker, and the wheels of His chariot speed on. Before He comes, a certain space must be gone over; all the Saints must be gathered in; and each Saint must be matured. Not a grain must fall to the ground; not an ear of corn must lose its due rain and sunshine. All we pray is, that He would please to crowd all this into a short space of time; that He would "finish the work and cut it short *in righteousness*," and "make a short work upon the earth;" that He would accomplish,—not curtail, but fulfil,—the

circle of His Saints, and hasten the age to come without disordering this. Indeed it cannot be otherwise. All God's works are in place and season; they are all complete. As in nature, the structure of its minutest portions is wrought out to perfection, and an insect is as wonderful as Leviathan; so, when in His providence He seems to hurry, He still keeps time, and moves upon the deep harmonies of truth and love. When then we pray that He would come, we pray also that we may be ready; that all things may converge and meet in Him; that He may draw us while He draws near us, and makes us the holier the closer He comes. We pray that we may not fear that which at present we justly do fear "that when He shall appear, we may have confidence, and not be ashamed before Him at His coming."[22] He can condense into an hour a life of trial. He who frames the worlds in a moment, and creates generations by the breath of His mouth, and melts, and hardens, and deluges, and dries up the solid rocks in a day, and makes bones to live, grow, and die, and buries them in the earth, and changes them into stone, apart from time and at His mere will, more wondrously can He deal with the world of spirits, who are never subject to the accidents of matter. He can by one keen pang of agony punish the earthly soul, or by one temptation justify it, or by one vision glorify it. Adam fell in a moment; Abraham was justified upon his seizing the knife; Moses lost Canaan for a word; David said, "I have sinned," and was forgiven; Solomon gained wisdom in a dream; Peter made one confession and received the

_____

[22] 1 John 2:28

keys; our Lord baffled Satan in three sentences; He redeemed us in the course of a day; He regenerates us by a form of words. We know not how "fearfully and wonderfully" our souls "are made." To men in sleep, in drowning, or in excitement, moments are as years. They suddenly become other men, nature or grace dispensing with time.

3. But again, you say, How can I pray to see Christ, who am so unclean? You say well that you are unclean. But in what time do you propose to become otherwise? Do you expect in this life ever to be clean? Yes, in one sense, by the presence of the Holy Ghost within you; but that presence we trust you have now. But if by "clean," you mean free from that infection of nature, the least drop of which is sufficient to dishonour all your services, clean you never will be till you have paid the debt of sin, and lose that body which Adam has begotten. Be sure that the longer you live, and the holier you become, you will only perceive that misery more clearly. The less of it you have, the more it will oppress you; its full draught does but confuse and stupify you; as you come to yourself, your misery begins. The more your soul becomes one with Him who deigns to dwell within it, the more it sees with His eyes. You dare not pray for His presence now;—would you pray for it had you lived Methuselah's years? I trow not. You will never be good enough to desire it; no one in the whole Church prays for it except on conditions implied. To the end of the longest life you are still a beginner. What Christ asks of you is not sinlessness, but diligence. Had you lived ten times your present age, ten times more service would be required of you. Every

day you live longer, more will be required. If He were to come today, you would be judged up to today. Did He come tomorrow, you would be judged up to tomorrow. Were the time put off a year, you would have a year more to answer for. You cannot elude your destiny, you cannot get rid of your talent; you are to answer for your opportunities, whatever they may be, not more nor less. You cannot be profitable to Him even with the longest life; you can show faith and love in an hour. True it is, if you have turned from Him, and served sin, and in proportion as you have done this, you have a great work before you,—to undo what you have done. If you have given years to Satan, you have a double duty, to repent as well as to work; but even then you may pray without dread; for in praying for His presence you still are praying, as I have said, to be ready for it.

4. But once more. You ask, how you can make up your mind to stand before your Lord and God; I ask in turn, how do you bring yourself to come before Him now day by day?—for what is this but meeting Him? Consider what it is you mean by praying, and you will see that, at that very time that you are asking for the coming of His kingdom, you are anticipating that coming, and accomplishing the thing you fear. When you pray, you come into His presence. Now reflect on yourself, what your feelings are in coming. They are these: you seem to say,—I am in myself nothing but a sinner, a man of unclean lips and earthly heart. I am not worthy to enter into His presence. I am not worthy of the least of all His mercies. I know He is All-holy, yet I come before Him; I place myself under His pure

and piercing eyes, which look me through and through, and discern every trace and every motion of evil within me. Why do I do so? First of all, for this reason. To whom should I go? What can I do better? Who is there in the whole world that can help me? Who that will care for me, or pity me, or have any kind thought of me, if I cannot obtain it of Him? I know He is of purer eyes than to behold iniquity; but I know again that He is All-merciful, and that He so sincerely desires my salvation that He has died for me. Therefore, though I am in a great strait, I will rather fall into His hands, than into those of any creature. True it is I could find creatures more like myself, imperfect or sinful: it might seem better to betake myself to some of these who have power with God, and to beseech them to interest themselves for me. But no; somehow I cannot content myself with this;—no, terrible as it is, I had rather go to God alone. I have an instinct within me which leads me to rise and go to my Father, to name the Name of His well-beloved Son, and having named it, to place myself unreservedly in His hands, saying, "If Thou, Lord, wilt be extreme to mark what is done amiss, O Lord, who may abide it! But there is forgiveness with Thee."—This is the feeling in which we come to confess our sins, and to pray to God for pardon and grace day by day; and observe, it is the very feeling in which we must prepare to meet Him when He comes visibly. Why, even children of this world can meet a judicial process and a violent death with firmness. I do not say that we must have aught of their pride or their self-trusting tranquillity. And yet there is a certain composure and dignity which become us who are born of immortal seed, when we come before our Father. If indeed we have habitually lived to the world, then truly it is natural we should attempt to fly from Him whom we have pierced. Then may we well call on the mountains to fall on us, and on the hills to cover us. But if we have lived, however imperfectly, yet habitually, in His fear, if we trust that His Spirit is in us, then we need not be ashamed before Him. We shall then come before Him, as now we come to pray—with profound abasement, with awe, with self-renunciation, still as relying upon the Spirit which He has given us, with our faculties about us, with a collected and determined mind, and with hope. He who cannot pray for Christ's coming, ought not in consistency to pray at all.

I have spoken of coming to God in prayer generally; but if this is awful, much more is coming to Him in the Sacrament of Holy Communion; for this is in very form an anticipation of His coming, a near presence of Him in earnest of it. And a number of men feel it to be so; for, for one reason or another, they never come before Him in that most Holy Ordinance, and so deprive themselves of the highest of blessings here below. Thus their feeling is much the same as theirs would be, who from fear of His coming, did not dare look out for it. They indeed who are in the religious practice of communicating, understand well enough how it is possible to feel afraid and yet to come. Surely it is possible, and the case is the same as regards the future day of Christ. You must tremble, and yet pray for it. We have all of us experienced enough even of this life, to know that the same seasons are often most joyful and also most painful. Instances of this must suggest themselves to all men. Consider the loss of friends, and say whether joy and grief, triumph and humiliation, are not strangely mingled, yet both really preserved. The joy does not change the grief, nor the grief the joy, into some third feeling; they are incommunicable with each other, both remain, both affect us. Or consider the mingled feelings with which a son obtains forgiveness of a father,—the soothing thought that all displeasure is at an end, the veneration, the love, and all the undescribable emotions, most pleasurable, which cannot be put into words,—yet his bitterness against himself. Such is the temper in which we desire to come to the Lord's table; such in which we must pray for His coming; such in which His elect will stand before Him when He comes.

5. Lastly, let me say more distinctly what I have already alluded to, that in that solemn hour we shall have, if we be His, the inward support of His Spirit too, carrying us on towards Him, and "witnessing with our spirits that we are the children of God." God is mysteriously threefold; and while He remains in the highest heaven, He comes to judge the world;—and while He judges the world, He is in us also, bearing us up and going forth in us to meet Himself. God the Son is without, but God the Spirit is within,—and when the Son asks, the Spirit will answer. That Spirit is vouchsafed to us here; and if we yield ourselves to His gracious influences, so that He draws up our thoughts and wills to heavenly things, and becomes one with us, He will assuredly be still in us and give us confidence at the Day of Judgment. He will be with us, and strengthen us; and how great His strength is, what mind

of man can conceive? Gifted with that supernatural strength, we may be able to lift up our eyes to our Judge when He looks on us, and look on Him in turn, though with deep awe, yet without confusion of face, as if in the consciousness of innocence.

That hour must come at length upon every one of us. When it comes, may the countenance of the Most Holy quicken, not consume us; may the flame of judgment be to us only what it was to the Three Holy Children, over whom the fire had no power!

Watching

*"Take ye heed, watch and pray; for ye know not
when the time is." Mark 13:33.*

Our Saviour gave this warning when He was leaving
this world,—leaving it, that is, as far as His visible
presence is concerned. He looked forward to the many
hundred years which were to pass before He came
again. He knew His own purpose and His Father's
purpose gradually to leave the world to itself, gradually
to withdraw from it the tokens of His gracious
presence. He contemplated, as contemplating all things,
the neglect of Him which would spread even among his
professed followers; the daring disobedience, and the
loud words, which would be ventured against Him and
His Father by many whom He had regenerated: and the
coldness, cowardice, and tolerance of error which
would be displayed by others, who did not go so far as
to speak or to act against Him. He foresaw the state of
the world and the Church, as we see it this day, when
His prolonged absence has made it practically thought,
that He never will come back in visible presence: and in
the text, He mercifully whispers into our ears, not to
trust in what we see, not to share in that general
unbelief, not to be carried away by the world, but to
"take heed, watch, pray," and look out for His coming.

Surely this gracious warning should be ever in our
thoughts, being so precise, so solemn, so earnest. He
foretold His first coming, yet He took His Church by
surprise when He came; much more will He come
suddenly the second time, and overtake men, now that

He has not measured out the interval before it, as then He did, but left our watchfulness to the keeping of faith and love.

Let us then consider this most serious question, which concerns every one of us so nearly;—What it is to *watch* for Christ? He says, "*Watch* ye therefore, for ye know not when the Master of the house cometh; at even, or at midnight, or at the cock-crowing, or in the morning; lest coming suddenly He find you sleeping. And what I say unto you, I say unto all, *Watch*." And again, "If the goodman of the house had known what hour the thief would come, he would have *watched*, and not have suffered his house to be broken through."[23] A like warning is given elsewhere both by our Lord and by His Apostles. For instance; we have the parable of the Ten Virgins, five of whom were wise and five foolish; on whom the bridegroom, after tarrying came suddenly, and five were found without oil. On which our Lord says, "*Watch* therefore, for ye know neither the day nor the hour wherein the Son of man cometh."[24] Again He says, "Take heed to yourselves, lest at any time your hearts be overcharged with surfeiting and drunkenness, and cares of this life, and so that day come upon you unawares; for as a snare shall it come on all them that dwell on the face of the whole earth. *Watch* ye therefore, and pray always, that ye may be accounted worthy to escape all these things that shall come to pass, and to stand before the Son of man."[25] In like

---

[23] Luke 12:39
[24] Matt. 25:13
[25] Luke 21:36

manner He upbraided Peter thus: "Simon, sleepest thou? couldest not thou *watch* one hour?"[26]

In like manner St. Paul in his Epistle to the Romans. "Now it is high time to awake out of sleep … The night is far spent, the day is at hand."[27] Again, "*Watch* ye, stand fast in the faith, quit you like men, be strong."[28] "Be strong in the Lord, and in the power of His might; put on the whole armour of God, that ye may be able to stand against the wiles of the devil… that ye may be able to withstand in the evil day, and having done all to stand."[29] "Let us not sleep as do others, but let us *watch* and be sober."[30] In like manner St. Peter, "The end of all things is at hand; be ye therefore sober, and *watch* unto prayer." "Be sober, be *vigilant*, because your adversary the devil, as a roaring lion, walketh about seeking whom he may devour." And St. John, "Behold I come as a thief; blessed is he that *watcheth* and keepeth his garments."[31]

Now I consider this word *watching*, first used by our Lord, then by the favoured Disciple, then by the two great Apostles, Peter and Paul, is a remarkable word, remarkable because the idea is not so obvious as might appear at first sight, and next because they all inculcate it. We are not simply to believe, but to watch; not simply to love, but to watch; not simply to obey, but to

[26] Mark 14:37
[27] Rom. 13:11-12
[28] 1 Cor. 16:13
[29] Eph. 6:10-13
[30] 1 Thess. 5:6
[31] Rev. 16:15

watch; to watch for what? for that great event, Christ's coming. Whether then we consider what is the obvious meaning of the word, or the Object towards which it directs us, we seem to see a special duty enjoined on us, such as does not naturally come into our minds. Most of us have a general idea what is meant by believing, fearing, loving, and obeying; but perhaps we do not contemplate or apprehend what is meant by watching.

And I conceive it is one of the main points, which, in a practical way, will be found to separate the true and perfect servants of God from the multitude called Christians; from those who are, I do not say false and reprobate, but who are such that we cannot speak much about them, nor can form any notion what will become of them. And in saying this, do not understand me as saying, which I do not, that we can tell for certain who are the perfect, and who the double-minded or incomplete Christians; or that those who discourse and insist upon these subjects are necessarily on the right side of the line. I am but speaking of two *characters*, the true and consistent character, and the inconsistent; and these I say will be found in no slight degree discriminated and distinguished by this one mark,—true Christians, whoever they are, watch, and inconsistent Christians do not. Now what is watching?

I conceive it may be explained as follows:—Do you know the feeling in matters of this life, of expecting a friend, expecting him to come, and he delays? Do you know what it is to be in unpleasant company, and to wish for the time to pass away, and the hour strike when you may be at liberty? Do you know what it is to be in anxiety lest something should happen which may happen or may not, or to be in suspense about some important event, which makes your heart beat when you are reminded of it, and of which you think the first thing in the morning? Do you know what it is to have a friend in a distant country, to expect news of him, and to wonder from day to day what he is now doing, and whether he is well? Do you know what it is so to live upon a person who is present with you, that your eyes follow his, that you read his soul, that you see all its changes in his countenance, that you anticipate his wishes, that you smile in his smile, and are sad in his sadness, and are downcast when he is vexed, and rejoice in his successes? To watch for Christ is a feeling such as all these; as far as feelings of this world are fit to shadow out those of another.

He watches for Christ who has a sensitive, eager, apprehensive mind; who is awake, alive, quick-sighted, zealous in seeking and honouring Him; who looks out for Him in all that happens, and who would not be surprised, who would not be over-agitated or overwhelmed, if he found that He was coming at once.

And he watches *with* Christ, who, while he looks on to the future, looks back on the past, and does not so contemplate what his Saviour has purchased for him, as to forget what He has suffered for him. He watches with Christ, who ever commemorates and renews in his own person Christ's Cross and Agony, and gladly takes up that mantle of affliction which Christ wore here, and left behind Him when he ascended. And hence in the Epistles, often as the inspired writers show their desire for His second coming, as often do they show their memory of His first, and never lose sight of His Crucifixion in His Resurrection. Thus if St. Paul reminds the Romans that they "wait for the redemption of the body" at the Last Day, he also says, "If so be that we *suffer with Him*, that we may be also glorified together." If he speaks to the Corinthians of "waiting for the coming of our Lord Jesus Christ," he also speaks of "always bearing about in the body the *dying* of the Lord Jesus, *that* the life also of Jesus might be made manifest in our body." If to the Philippians of "the power of His resurrection," he adds at once "*and the fellowship of His sufferings*, being made conformable unto His death." If he consoles the Colossians with the hope "when Christ shall appear," of their "appearing with Him in glory," he has already declared that he "*fills up that which remains of the afflictions of Christ* in his flesh for His body's sake, which is the Church."[32] Thus the thought of what Christ is, must not obliterate from the mind the thought of what He was; and faith is always sorrowing with Him while it rejoices. And the same union of opposite thoughts is impressed on us in Holy Communion, in which we see Christ's death and resurrection together, at one and the same time; we commemorate the one, we rejoice in the other; we make an offering, and we gain a blessing.

This then is to watch; to be detached from what is present, and to live in what is unseen; to live in the thought of Christ as He came once, and as He will

---

[32] Rom. 8:17-28; 1 Cor. 1:7; 2 Cor. 4:10; Phil. 3:10; Col. 3:4; Col. 1:24

come again; to desire His second coming, from our affectionate and grateful remembrance of His first. And this it is, in which we shall find that men in general are wanting. They are indeed without faith and love also; but at least they profess to have these graces, nor is it easy to convince them that they have not. For they consider they have faith, if they do but own that the Bible came from God, or that they trust wholly in Christ for salvation; and they consider they have love if they obey some of the most obvious of God's commandments. Love and faith they think they have; but surely they do not even fancy that they watch. What is meant by watching, and how it is a duty, they have no definite idea; and thus it accidentally happens that watching is a suitable test of a Christian, in that it is that particular property of faith and love, which, essential as it is, men of this world do not even profess; that particular property, which is the life or energy of faith and love, the way in which faith and love, if genuine, show themselves.

It is easy to exemplify what I mean, from the experience which we all have of life. Many men indeed are open revilers of religion, or at least openly disobey its laws; but let us consider those who are of a more sober and conscientious cast of mind. They have a number of good qualities, and are in a certain sense and up to a certain point religious; but they do not watch. Their notion of religion is briefly this: loving God indeed, but loving this world too; not only doing their *duty*, but finding their chief and highest *good*, in that state of life to which it has pleased God to call them, resting in it, taking it as their portion. They serve God, and they seek Him; but they look on the present world as if it were the eternal, not a mere temporary, scene of their duties and privileges, and never contemplate the prospect of being separated from it. It is not that they forget God, or do not live by principle, or forget that the goods of this world are His gift; but they love them for their own sake more than for the sake of the Giver, and reckon on their remaining, as if they had that permanence which their duties and religious privileges have. They do not understand that they are called to be strangers and pilgrims upon the earth, and that their worldly lot and worldly goods are a sort of accident of their existence, and that they really have no property, though human law guarantees property to them. Accordingly, they set their heart upon their goods, be they great or little, not without a sense of religion the while, but still idolatrously. *This* is their fault,—an identifying God with this world, and therefore an idolatry towards this world; and so they are rid of the trouble of looking out for their God, for they think they have found Him in the goods of this world. While, then, they are really praiseworthy in many parts of their conduct, benevolent, charitable, kind, neighbourly, and useful in their generation, nay, constant perhaps in the ordinary religious duties which custom has established, and while they display much right and amiable feeling, and much correctness in opinion, and are even in the way to improve in character and conduct as time goes on, correct much that is amiss, gain greater command over themselves, mature in judgment, and are much looked up to in consequence; yet still it is plain that they love this world, would be loth to leave it, and wish to have more of its good things. They like wealth, and distinction, and credit, and influence. They may improve in conduct, but not in aims; they advance, but they do not mount; they are moving on a low level, and were they to move on for centuries, would never rise above the atmosphere of this world. "I will stand upon my watch, and set me upon the tower, and will watch to see what He will say unto me, and what I shall answer when I am reproved."[33] This is the temper of mind which they have not; and when we reflect how rarely it *is* found among professing Christians, we shall see why our Lord is so urgent in enforcing it;—as if He said, "I am not warning you, My followers, against open apostasy; that will not be; but I foresee that very few will keep awake and watch while I am away. Blessed are the servants who do so; few will open to me *immediately*, when I knock. They will have something to do first; they will have to get ready. They will have to recover from the surprise and confusion which overtake them on the first news of My coming, and will need time to collect themselves, and summon about them their better thoughts and affections. They feel themselves very well off as they are; and wish to serve God as they are. They are satisfied to remain on earth; they do not wish to move; they do not wish to change."

Without denying, then, to these persons the praise of many religious habits and practices, I would say that they want the tender and sensitive heart which hangs on the thought of Christ, and lives in His love. The breath of the world has a peculiar power in what may be called

---

[33] Hab. 2:1

rusting the soul. The mirror within them, instead of reflecting back the Son of God their Saviour, has become dim and discoloured; and hence, though (to use a common expression) they have a good deal of good *in* them, it is only *in* them, it is not through them, around them, and upon them. An evil crust is *on* them: they think with the world; they are full of the world's notions and modes of speaking; they appeal to the world, and have a sort of reverence for what the world will say. There is a want of naturalness, simplicity, and childlike teachableness in them. It is difficult to touch them, or (what may be called) get at them, and to persuade them to a straight-forward course in religion. They start off when you least expect it: they have reservations, make distinctions, take exceptions, indulge in refinements, in questions where there are really but two sides, a right and a wrong. Their religious feelings do not flow forth easily, at times when they ought to flow; either they are diffident, and can say nothing, or else they are affected and strained in their mode of conversing. And as a rust preys upon metal and eats into it, so does this worldly spirit penetrate more and more deeply into the soul which once admits it. And this is one great end, as it would appear, of afflictions, viz., to rub away and clear off these outward defilements, and to keep the soul in a measure of its baptismal purity and brightness.

Now, it cannot surely be doubted that multitudes in the Church are such as I have been describing, and that they would not, could not, at once welcome our Lord on His coming. We cannot, indeed, apply what has been said to this or that individual; but on the whole, viewing the multitude, one cannot be mistaken. There may be exceptions; but after all conceivable deductions, a large body must remain thus double-minded, thus attempting to unite things incompatible. This we might be sure of, though Christ had said nothing on the subject; but it is a most affecting and solemn thought, that He has actually called our attention to this very danger, the danger of a worldly religiousness, for so it may be called, though it *is* religiousness; this mixture of religion and unbelief, which serves God indeed, but loves the fashions, the distinctions, the pleasures, the comforts of this life,—which feels a satisfaction in being prosperous in circumstances, likes pomps and vanities, is particular about food, raiment, house, furniture, and domestic matters, courts great people, and aims at having a position in society. He warns His disciples of the danger of having their minds drawn off from the thought of Him, by whatever cause; He warns them against *all* excitements, *all* allurements of this world; He solemnly warns them that the world will not be prepared for His coming, and tenderly intreats of them not to take their portion with the world. He warns them by the instance of the rich man whose soul was required, of the servant who ate and drank, and of the foolish virgins. When He comes, they will one and all want time; their head will be confused, their eyes will swim, their tongue falter, their limbs totter, as men who are suddenly awakened. They will not all at once collect their senses and faculties. O fearful thought! the bridal train is sweeping by,—Angels are there,—the just made perfect are there,—little children, and holy teachers, and white-robed saints, and martyrs washed in blood; the marriage of the Lamb is come, and His wife hath made herself ready. She has already attired herself: while we have been sleeping, she has been robing; she has been adding jewel to jewel, and grace to grace; she has been gathering in her chosen ones, one by one, and has been exercising them in holiness, and purifying them for her Lord; and now her marriage hour is come. The holy Jerusalem is descending, and a loud voice proclaims, "Behold, the bridegroom cometh; go ye out to meet Him!" but we, alas! are but dazzled with the blaze of light, and neither welcome the sound, nor obey it,—and all for what? what shall we have gained then? what will this world have then done for us? wretched, deceiving world! which will then be burned up, unable not only to profit us, but to save itself. Miserable hour, indeed, will that be, when the full consciousness breaks on us of what we will not believe now, viz., that we *are* at present serving the world. We trifle with our conscience now; we deceive our better judgment; we repel the hints of those who tell us that we are joining ourselves to this perishing world. We *will* taste a little of its pleasures, and follow its ways, and think it no harm, so that we do not altogether neglect religion. I mean, we allow ourselves to covet what we have not, to boast in what we have, to look down on those who have less; or we allow ourselves to profess what we do not try to practise, to argue for the sake of victory, and to debate when we should be obeying; and we pride ourselves on our reasoning powers, and think ourselves enlightened, and despise those who had less to say for themselves, and set forth and defend our own theories; or we are over-anxious, fretful, and care-worn about worldly matters, spiteful, envious, jealous, discontented, and evil-natured: in one or other way we take our portion with this world, and we will not believe that we do. We obstinately refuse to believe it; we know we are not altogether irreligious, and we persuade ourselves that we are religious. We learn to think it is possible to be too religious; we have taught ourselves that there is nothing high or deep in religion, no great exercise of our affections, no great food for our thoughts, no great work for our exertions. We go on in a self-satisfied or a self-conceited way, not looking out of ourselves, not standing like soldiers on the watch in the dark night; but we kindle our own fire, and delight ourselves in the sparks of it. This is our state, or something like this, and the Day will declare it; the Day is at hand, and the Day will search our hearts, and bring it home even to ourselves, that we have been cheating ourselves with words, and have not served Christ, as the Redeemer of the soul claims, but with a meagre, partial, worldly service, and without really contemplating Him who is above and apart from this world.

Year passes after year silently; Christ's coming is ever nearer than it was. O that, as He comes nearer earth, we may approach nearer heaven! O, my brethren, pray Him to give you the heart to seek Him in sincerity. Pray Him to make you in earnest. You have one work only, to bear your cross after Him. Resolve in His strength to do so. Resolve to be no longer beguiled by "shadows of religion," by words, or by disputings, or by notions, or by high professions, or by excuses, or by the world's promises or threats. Pray Him to give you what Scripture calls "an honest and good heart," or "a perfect heart," and, without waiting, begin at once to obey Him with the best heart you have. Any obedience is better than none,—any profession which is disjoined from obedience, is a mere pretence and deceit. Any religion which does not bring you nearer to God is of the world. You have to seek His face; obedience is the only way of seeking Him. All your duties are obediences. If you are to believe the truths He has revealed, to regulate yourselves by His precepts, to be frequent in His ordinances, to adhere to His Church and people, why is it, except because *He* has bid you? and to do what He bids is to obey Him, and to obey Him is to approach Him. Every act of obedience is an approach,—an approach to Him who is not far off, though He seems so, but close behind this visible screen of things which hides Him from us. He is behind this material framework; earth and sky are but a veil going between Him and us; the day will come when He will rend that veil, and show Himself to us. And then, according as we have waited for Him, will He recompense us. If we have forgotten Him, He will not know us; but "blessed are those servants whom the Lord, when He cometh, shall find watching … He shall gird Himself, and make them sit down to meat, and will come forth and serve them. And if He shall come in the second watch, or come in the third watch, and find them so, blessed are those servants,"[34] May this be the portion of every one of us! It is hard to attain it; but it is woeful to fail. Life is short; death is certain; and the world to come is everlasting.

---

[34] Luke 12:37-38

CHRISTMAS

The Incarnation

"The Word was made flesh, and dwelt among us." John 1:14.

Thus does the favoured Apostle and Evangelist announce to us that Sacred Mystery, which we this day especially commemorate, the incarnation of the Eternal Word. Thus briefly and simply does he speak as if fearing he should fail in fitting reverence. If any there was who might seem to have permission to indulge in words on this subject, it was the beloved disciple, who had heard and seen, and looked upon, and handled the Word of Life; yet, in proportion to the height of his privilege, was his discernment of the infinite distance between him and his Creator. Such too was the temper of the Holy Angels, when the Father "brought in the First-begotten into the world:"[35] they straightway worshipped Him. And such was the feeling of awe and love mingled together, which remained for a while in the Church after Angels had announced His coming, and Evangelists had recorded His sojourn here, and His departure; "there was silence as it were for half an hour."[36] Around the Church, indeed, the voices of blasphemy were heard, even as when He hung on the cross; but in the Church there was light and peace, fear, joy, and holy meditation. Lawless doubtings, importunate inquirings, confident reasonings were not. An heartfelt adoration, a practical devotion to the Ever-

---

[35] Heb. 1:6
[36] Rev. 8:1

blessed Son, precluded difficulties in faith, and sheltered the Church from the necessity of speaking.

He who had seen the Lord Jesus with a pure mind, attending Him from the Lake of Gennesareth to Calvary, and from the Sepulchre to Mount Olivet, where He left this scene of His humiliation; he who had been put in charge with His Virgin Mother, and heard from her what she alone could tell of the Mystery to which she had ministered; and they who had heard it from his mouth, and those again whom these had taught, the first generations of the Church, needed no explicit declarations concerning His Sacred Person. Sight and hearing superseded the multitude of words; faith dispensed with the aid of lengthened Creeds and Confessions. There was silence. "The Word was made flesh;" "I believe in Jesus Christ His only Son our Lord;" sentences such as these conveyed everything, yet were officious in nothing. But when the light of His advent faded, and love waxed cold, then there was an opening for objection and discussion, and a difficulty in answering. Then misconceptions had to be explained, doubts allayed, questions set at rest, innovators silenced. Christians were forced to speak against their will, lest heretics should speak instead of them.

Such is the difference between our own state and that of the early Church, which the present Festival especially brings to mind. In the New Testament we find the doctrine of the Incarnation announced clearly indeed, but with a reverent brevity. "The Word was made flesh," "God was manifest in the flesh." "God was in Christ." "Unto us a Child is born,—the mighty

God." "Christ, over all, God, blessed for ever." "My Lord and my God." "I am Alpha and Omega, the beginning and the ending,—the Almighty." "The Son of God, the brightness of His glory, and the express image of His person."[37] But we are obliged to speak more at length in the Creeds and in our teaching, to meet the perverse ingenuity of those who, when the Apostles were removed, could with impunity insult and misinterpret the letter of their writings.

Nay, further, so circumstanced are we, as to be obliged not only thus to guard the Truth, but even to give the reason of our guarding it. For they who would steal away the Lord from us, not content with forcing us to measures of protection, even go on to bring us to account for adopting them; and demand that we should put aside whatever stands between them and their heretical purposes. Therefore it is necessary to state clearly, as I have already done, why the Church has lengthened her statements of Christian doctrine. Another reason of these statements is as follows: time having proceeded, and the true traditions of our Lord's ministry being lost to us, the Object of our faith is but faintly reflected on our minds, compared with the vivid picture which His presence impressed upon the early Christians. True is it the Gospels will do very much by way of realizing for us the incarnation of the Son of God, if studied in faith and love. But the Creeds are an additional help this way. The declarations made in them, the distinctions, cautions, and the like, supported and

---

[37] 1 Tim. 3:16; 2 Cor. 5:19; Isa. 9:6; Rom. 9:5; John 20:28; Rev. 1:8; Heb. 1:2-3

illuminated by Scripture, draw down, as it were, from heaven, the image of Him who is on God's right hand, preserve us from an indolent use of words without apprehending them, and rouse in us those mingled feelings of fear and confidence, affection and devotion towards Him, which are implied in the belief of a personal advent of God in our nature, and which were originally derived to the Church from the very sight of Him.

And we may say further still, these statements—such, for instance, as occur in the Te Deum and Athanasian Creed—are especially suitable in divine worship, inasmuch as they kindle and elevate the religious affections. They are hymns of praise and thanksgiving; they give glory to God as revealed in the Gospel, just as David's Psalms magnify His Attributes as displayed in nature, His wonderful works in the creation of the world, and His mercies towards the house of Israel.

With these objects, then, it may be useful, on today's Festival, to call your attention to the Catholic doctrine of the Incarnation.

The Word was from the beginning, the Only-begotten Son of God. Before all worlds were created, while as yet time was not, He was in existence, in the bosom of the Eternal Father, God from God, and Light from Light, supremely blessed in knowing and being known of Him, and receiving all divine perfections from Him, yet ever One with Him who begat Him. As it is said in the opening of the Gospel: "In the beginning was the Word, and the Word was with God, and the Word was God." If we may dare conjecture, He is called the Word of God, as mediating between the Father and all creatures; bringing them into being, fashioning them, giving the world its laws, imparting reason and conscience to creatures of a higher order, and revealing to them in due season the knowledge of God's will. And to us Christians He is especially the Word in that great mystery commemorated today, whereby He became flesh, and redeemed us from a state of sin.

He, indeed, when man fell, might have remained in the glory which He had with the Father before the world was. But that unsearchable Love, which showed itself in our original creation, rested not content with a frustrated work, but brought Him down again from His Father's bosom to do His will, and repair the evil which sin had caused. And with a wonderful condescension He came, not as before in power, but in weakness, in the form of a servant, in the likeness of that fallen creature whom He purposed to restore. So He humbled Himself; suffering all the infirmities of our nature in the likeness of sinful flesh, all but a sinner,—pure from all sin, yet subjected to all temptation,—and at length becoming obedient unto death, even the death of the cross.

I have said that when the Only-begotten Son stooped to take upon Him our nature, He had no fellowship with sin. It was impossible that He should. Therefore, since our nature was corrupt since Adam's fall, He did not come in the way of nature, He did not clothe Himself in that corrupt flesh which Adam's race inherits. He came by miracle, so as to take on Him our imperfection without having any share in our sinfulness. He was not born as other men are; for "that which is born of the flesh is flesh."[38]

All Adam's children are children of wrath; so our Lord came as the Son of Man, but not the son of sinful Adam. He had no earthly father; He abhorred to have one. The thought may not be suffered that He should have been the son of shame and guilt. He came by a new and living way; not, indeed, formed out of the ground, as Adam was at the first, lest He should miss the participation of our nature, but selecting and purifying unto Himself a tabernacle out of that which existed. As in the beginning, woman was formed out of man by Almighty power, so now, by a like mystery, but a reverse order, the new Adam was fashioned from the woman. He was, as had been foretold, the immaculate "seed of the woman," deriving His manhood from the substance of the Virgin Mary; as it is expressed in the articles of the Creed, "conceived by the Holy Ghost, born of the Virgin Mary."

Thus the Son of God became the Son of Man; mortal, but not a sinner; heir of our infirmities, not of our guiltiness; the offspring of the old race, yet "the beginning of the" new "creation of God." Mary, His mother, was a sinner as others, and born of sinners; but she was set apart, "as a garden inclosed, a spring shut up, a fountain sealed," to yield a created nature to Him who was her Creator. Thus He came into this world, not in the clouds of heaven, but born into it, born of a

---

[38] John 3:6

woman; He, the Son of Mary, and she (if it may be said), the mother of God. Thus He came, selecting and setting apart for Himself the elements of body and soul; then, uniting them, to Himself from their first origin of existence, pervading them, hallowing them by His own Divinity, spiritualizing them, and filling them with light and purity, the while they continued to be human, and for a time mortal and exposed to infirmity. And, as they grew from day to day in their holy union, His Eternal Essence still was one with them, exalting them, acting in them, manifesting Itself through them, so that He was truly God and Man, One Person,—as we are soul and body, yet one man, so truly God and man are not two, but One Christ. Thus did the Son of God enter this mortal world; and when He had reached man's estate, He began His ministry, preached the Gospel, chose His Apostles, suffered on the cross, died, and was buried, rose again and ascended on high, there to reign till the day when He comes again to judge the world. This is the All-gracious Mystery of the Incarnation, good to look into, good to adore; according to the saying in the text, "The Word was made flesh,—and dwelt among us."

The brief account thus given of the Catholic doctrine of the incarnation of the Eternal Word, may be made more distinct by referring to some of those modes mentioned in Scripture, in which God has at divers times condescended to manifest Himself in His creatures, which come short of it.

1. God was in the Prophets, but not as He was in Christ. The divine authority, and in one sense, name,

may be given to His Ministers, considered as His representatives. Moses says to the Israelites, "Your murmurings are not against us, but against the Lord." And St. Paul, "He therefore that despiseth, despiseth not man, but God."[39] In this sense, Rulers and Judges are sometimes called gods, as our Lord Himself says.

And further, the Prophets were inspired. Thus John the Baptist is said to have been filled with the Holy Ghost from his mother's womb. Zacharias was filled with the Holy Ghost, and prophesied. In like manner the Holy Ghost came on the Apostles at Pentecost and at other times; and so wonderfully gifted was St. Paul, that "from his body were brought unto the sick handkerchiefs or aprons, and the diseases departed from them, and the evil spirits went out of them." [40] Now the characteristic of this miraculous inspiration was, that the presence of God came and went. Thus we read, in the afore-mentioned and similar narratives, of the Prophet or Apostle being *filled* with the Spirit on particular occasions; as again of "the Spirit of the Lord departing from Saul," and an evil spirit troubling him. Thus this divine inspiration was so far parallel to demoniacal possession. We find in the Gospels the devil speaking with the voice of his victim, so that the tormentor and the tormented could not be distinguished from each other. They seemed to be one and the same, though they were not; as appeared when Christ and His Apostles cast the devil out. And so again the Jewish Temple was in one sense inhabited by the

---

[39] Exod. 16:8; 1 Thess. 4:8
[40] Acts 19:12

presence of God, which came down upon it at Solomon's Prayer. This was a type of our Lord's manhood dwelt in by the Word of God as a Temple; still, with this essential difference, that the Jewish Temple was perishable, and again the Divine Presence might recede from it. There was no real unity between the one and the other; they were separable. But Christ says to the Jews of His own body, "Destroy this Temple and I will raise it in three days;" implying in these words such an unity between the Godhead and the manhood, that there could be no real separation, no dissolution. Even when His body was dead, the Divine Nature was one with it; in like manner it was one with His soul in paradise. Soul and body were really one with the Eternal Word,—not one in name only,—one never to be divided. Therefore Scripture says that He rose again "according to the Spirit of holiness;" and "that it was not possible that He should be holden of death."[41]

2. Again, the Gospel teaches us another mode in which man may be said to be united with Almighty God. It is the peculiar blessedness of the Christian, as St. Peter tells us, to be "partaker of the Divine Nature." [42] We believe, and have joy in believing, that the grace of Christ renews our carnal souls, repairing the effects of Adam's fall. Where Adam brought in impurity and unbelief, the power of God infuses faith and holiness. Thus we have God's perfections communicated to us anew, and, as being under immediate heavenly influences, are said to be one with God. And further,

---

[41] Rom. 1:4; Acts 2:24
[42] 2 Pet. 1:4

we are assured of some real though mystical fellowship with the Father, Son, and Holy Spirit, in order to this: so that both by a real presence in the soul, and by the fruits of grace, God is one with every believer, as in a consecrated Temple. But still, inexpressible as is this gift of Divine Mercy, it were blasphemy not to say that the indwelling of the Father in the Son is infinitely above this, being quite different in kind; for He is not merely of a divine nature, divine by participation of holiness and perfection, but Life and Holiness itself, such as the Father is,—the Co-eternal Son incarnate, God clothed with our nature, the Word made flesh.

3. And lastly, we read in the Patriarchal History of various appearances of Angels so remarkable that we can scarcely hesitate to suppose them to be gracious visions of the Eternal Son. For instance; it is said that "the Angel of the Lord appeared unto" Moses "in a flame of fire out of the midst of a bush;" yet presently this supernatural Presence is called "the Lord," and afterwards reveals His name to Moses, as "the God of Abraham, Isaac, and Jacob." On the other hand, St. Stephen speaks of Him as "the Angel which appeared to Moses in the bush." Again, he says soon after, that Moses was "in the Church in the wilderness with the Angel which spake to him in the mount Sinai;" yet in the book of Exodus we read, "Moses went up unto God, and the Lord called unto him out of the mountain;" "God spake all these words saying;" and the like.[43] Now, assuming, as we seem to have reason to assume, that the Son of God is herein revealed to us as

---

[43] Exod. 3:2; Acts 7:35-38; Exod. 29:3; Exod. 20:1

graciously ministering to the Patriarchs, Moses, and others, in angelic form, the question arises, what was the nature of this appearance? We are not informed, nor may we venture to determine; still, any how, the Angel was but the temporary outward form which the Eternal Word assumed, whether it was of a material nature, or a vision. Whether or no it was really an Angel, or but an appearance existing only for the immediate purpose, still, any how, we could not with propriety say that our Lord "took upon Him the nature of Angels."

Now these instances of the indwelling of Almighty God in a created substance, which I have given by way of contrast to that infinitely higher and mysterious union which is called the Incarnation, actually supply the senses in which heretics at various times have perverted our holy and comfortable doctrine, and which have obliged us to have recourse to Creeds and Confessions. Rejecting the teaching of the Church, and dealing rudely with the Word of God, they have ventured to deny that "Jesus Christ is come in the flesh," pretending He merely showed Himself as a vision or phantom;—or they have said that the Word of God merely dwelt in the man Christ Jesus, as the Shechinah in the Temple, having no real union with the Son of Mary (as if there were two distinct Beings, the Word and Jesus, even as the blessed Spirit is distinct from a man's soul);—or that Christ was called God for His great spiritual perfections, and that He gradually attained them by long practice. All these are words not to be uttered, except to show what the true doctrine is, and what is the meaning of the language of the Church concerning it. For instance, the Athanasian Creed confesses that Christ is "God of the substance of the Father, begotten before the worlds, perfect God," lest we should consider His Divine Nature, like ours, as merely a nature resembling God's holiness: that He is "Man of the substance of His Mother, born in the world, perfect man," lest we should think of Him as "not come in the flesh," a mere Angelic vision; and that "although He be God and man, yet He is not two, but one Christ," lest we should fancy that the Word of God entered into Him and then departed, as the Holy Ghost in the Prophets.

Such are the terms in which we are constrained to speak of our Lord and Saviour, by the craftiness of His enemies and our own infirmity; and we intreat His leave to do so. We intreat His leave, not as if forgetting that a reverent silence is best on so sacred a subject; but, when evil men and seducers abound on every side, and our own apprehensions of the Truth are dull, using zealous David's argument, "Is there not a cause" for words? We intreat His leave, and we humbly pray that what was first our defence against pride and indolence, may become an outlet of devotion, a service of worship. Nay, we surely trust that He will accept mercifully what we offer in faith, "doing what we can;" though the ointment of spikenard which we pour out is nothing to that true Divine Glory which manifested itself in Him, when the Holy Ghost singled Him out from other men, and the Father's voice acknowledged Him as His dearly beloved Son. Surely He will mercifully accept it, if faith offers what the intellect provides; if love kindles the sacrifice, zeal fans it, and reverence guards it. He will illuminate our earthly words from His own Divine Holiness, till they become saving truths to the souls which trust in Him. He who turned water into wine, and (did He so choose) could make bread of the hard stone, will sustain us for a brief season on this mortal fare. And we, while we make use of it, will never so forget its imperfection, as not to look out constantly for the True Beatific Vision; never so perversely remember that imperfection as to reject what is necessary for our present need. The time will come, if we be found worthy, when we, who now see in a glass darkly, shall see our Lord and Saviour face to face; shall behold His countenance beaming with the fulness of Divine Perfections, and bearing its own witness that He is the Son of God. We shall see Him as He is.

Let us then, according to the light given us, praise and bless Him in the Church below, whom Angels in heaven see and adore. Let us bless Him for His surpassing loving-kindness in taking upon Him our infirmities to redeem us, when He dwelt in the inner-most love of the Everlasting Father, in the glory which He had with Him before the world was. He came in lowliness and want; born amid the tumults of a mixed and busy multitude, cast aside into the outhouse of a crowded inn, laid to His first rest among the brute cattle. He grew up, as if the native of a despised city, and was bred to a humble craft. He bore to live in a world that slighted Him, for He lived in it, in order in due time to die for it. He came as the appointed Priest, to offer sacrifice for those who took no part in the act of worship; He came to offer up for sinners that precious blood which was meritorious by virtue of His

Divine Anointing. He died, to rise again the third day, the Sun of Righteousness, fully displaying that splendour which had hitherto been concealed by the morning clouds. He rose again, to ascend to the right hand of God, there to plead His sacred wounds in token of our forgiveness, to rule and guide His ransomed people, and from His pierced side to pour forth his choicest blessings upon them. He ascended, thence to descend again in due season to judge the world which He has redeemed.—Great is our Lord, and great is His power, Jesus the Son of God and Son of man. Ten thousand times more dazzling bright than the highest Archangel, is our Lord and Christ. By birth the Only-begotten and Express image of God; and in taking our flesh, not sullied thereby, but raising human nature with Him, as He rose from the lowly manger to the right hand of power,—raising human nature, for Man has redeemed us, Man is set above all creatures, as one with the Creator, Man shall judge man at the last day. So honoured is this earth, that no stranger shall judge us, but He who is our fellow, who will sustain our interests, and has full sympathy in all our imperfections. He who loved us, even to die for us, is graciously appointed to assign the final measurement and price upon His own work. He who best knows by infirmity to take the part of the infirm, He who would fain reap the full fruit of His passion, He will separate the wheat from the chaff, so that not a grain shall fall to the ground. He who has given us to share His own spiritual nature, He from whom we have drawn the life's blood of our souls, He our brother will decide about His brethren. In that His second coming, may He in His grace and loving pity remember us, who is our only hope, our only salvation!

Christ Hidden from the World
(Preached on Christmas Day)

"The light shineth in darkness, and the darkness comprehended it not." John 1:5.

Of all the thoughts which rise in the mind when contemplating the sojourn of our Lord Jesus Christ upon earth, none perhaps is more affecting and subduing than the obscurity which attended it. I do not mean His obscure condition, in the sense of its being humble; but the obscurity in which He was shrouded, and the secrecy which He observed. This characteristic of His first Advent is referred to very frequently in Scripture, as in the text, "The light shineth in darkness, and the darkness comprehended it not;" and is in contrast with what is foretold about His second Advent. Then "every eye shall see Him;" which implies that all shall recognize Him; whereas, when He came for the first time, though many saw Him, few indeed discerned Him. It had been prophesied, "When we shall see Him there is no beauty that we should desire Him;" and at the very end of his ministry, He said to one of His twelve chosen friends, "Have I been so long time with you, and yet hast thou not known Me, Philip?"[44]

I propose to set before you one or two thoughts which arise from this very solemn circumstance, and which may, through God's blessing, be profitable.

---

[44] Isai. 53:2; John 14:9

1. And first, let us review some of the circumstances which marked His sojourn when on earth.

His condescension in coming down from heaven, in leaving His Father's glory and taking flesh, is so far beyond power of words or thought, that one might consider at first sight that it mattered little whether He came as a prince or a beggar. And yet after all, it *is* much more wonderful that He came in low estate, for this reason; because it might have been thought beforehand, that, though He condescended to come on earth, yet He would not submit to be overlooked and despised: now the rich are not despised by the world, and the poor are. If He had come as a great prince or noble, the world without knowing a whit more that He was God, yet would at least have looked up to Him and honoured Him, as being a prince; but when He came in a low estate, He took upon him one additional humiliation, *contempt*,—being contemned, scorned, rudely passed by, roughly profaned by His creatures.

What were the actual circumstances of His coming? His Mother is a poor woman; she comes to Bethlehem to be taxed, travelling, when her choice would have been to remain at home. She finds there is no room in the inn; she is obliged to betake herself to a stable; she brings forth her firstborn Son, and lays Him in a manger. That little babe, so born, so placed, is none other than the Creator of heaven and earth, the Eternal Son of God.

Well; He was born of a poor woman, laid in a manger, brought up to a lowly trade, that of a carpenter; and when He began to preach the Gospel He had not a place to lay His head: lastly, He was put to death, to an infamous and odious death, the death which criminals then suffered.

For the three last years of His life, He preached the Gospel, I say, as we read in Scripture; but He did not begin to do so till He was thirty years old. For the first thirty years of His life, He seems to have lived, just as a poor man would live now. Day after day, season after season, winter and summer, one year and then another, passed on, as might happen to any of us. He passed from being a babe in arms to being a child, and then He became a boy, and so He grew up "like a tender plant," increasing in wisdom and stature; and then He seems to have followed the trade of Joseph, His reputed father; going on in an ordinary way without any great occurrence, till He was thirty years old. How very wonderful is all this! that He should live here, doing nothing great, so long; living here, as if for the sake of living; not preaching, or collecting disciples, or apparently in any way furthering the cause which brought Him down from heaven. Doubtless there were deep and wise reasons in God's counsels for His going on so long in obscurity; I only mean, that *we* do not know them.

And it is remarkable that those who were about Him, seem to have treated Him as one of their equals. His brethren, that is, His near relations, His cousins, did not believe in him. And it is very observable, too, that when He began to preach and a multitude collected, we are told, "When His friends heard of it they went out to lay hold on Him; for they said, He is beside himself."[45] They treated Him as we might be disposed, and rightly, to treat any ordinary person now, who began to preach in the streets. I say "rightly," because such persons generally preach a *new* Gospel, and therefore must be wrong. Also, they preach without being sent, and against authority; all which is wrong too. Accordingly we are often tempted to say that such people are "beside themselves," or mad, and not unjustly. It is often charitable to say so, for it is better to be mad than to be disobedient. Well, what we should say of such persons, this is what our Lord's friends said of Him. They had lived so long with Him, and yet did not know Him; did not understand what He was. They saw nothing to mark a difference between Him and them. He was dressed as others, He ate and drank as others, He came in and went out, and spoke, and walked, and slept, as others. He was in all respects a man, except that He did not sin; and this great difference the many would not detect, because none of us understands those who are much better than himself: so that Christ, the sinless Son of God, might be living close to us, and we not discover it.

2. I say that Christ, the sinless Son of God, might be living now in the world as our next door neighbour, and perhaps we not find it out. And this is a thought that should be dwelt on. I do not mean to say that there are not a number of persons, who we could be sure were not Christ; of course, no persons who lead bad and irreligious lives. But there are a number of persons who

---

45 Mark 3:21

are in no sense irreligious, or open to serious blame, who are very much like each other at first sight, yet in God's eyes are very different. I mean the great mass of what are called respectable men, who vary very much: some are merely decent and outwardly correct persons, and have no great sense of religion, do not deny themselves, have no ardent love of God, but love the world; and, whereas their interest lies in being regular and orderly, or they have no strong passions, or have early got into the way of being regular, and their habits are formed accordingly, they are what they are, decent and correct, but very little more. But there are others who look just the same to the world, who in their hearts are very different; they make no great show, they go on in the same quiet ordinary way as the others, but really they are training to be saints in Heaven. They do all they can to change themselves, to become like God, to obey God, to discipline themselves, to renounce the world; but they do it in secret, both because God tells them so to do, and because they do not like it to be known. Moreover, there are a number of others between these two with more or less of worldliness and more or less of faith. Yet they all look about the same, to common eyes, because true religion is a hidden life in the heart; and though it cannot exist without deeds, yet these are for the most part secret deeds, secret charities, secret prayers, secret self-denials, secret struggles, secret victories.

Of course in proportion as persons are brought out into public life, they will be seen and scrutinized, and (in a certain sense) known more; but I am talking of the ordinary condition of people in private life, such as our

Saviour was for thirty years; and these look very like each other. And there are so many of them, that unless we get very near them, we cannot see any distinction between one and another; we have no means to do so, and it is no business of ours. And yet, though we have no right to judge others, but must leave this to God, it is very certain that a really holy man, a true saint, though he looks like other men, still has a sort of secret power in him to attract others to him who are like-minded, and to influence all who have any thing in them like him. And thus it often becomes a test, whether we are like-minded with the Saints of God, whether they have influence over us. And though we have no means of knowing at the time who are God's own Saints, yet after all is over we have; and then on looking back on what is past, perhaps after they are dead and gone, if we knew them, we may ask ourselves what power they had over us, whether they attracted us, influenced us, humbled us, whether they made our hearts burn within us. Alas! too often we shall find that we were close to them for a long time, had means of knowing them, and knew them not; and that is a heavy condemnation on us, indeed. Now this was singularly exemplified in our Saviour's history, by how much He was so very holy. The holier a man is, the less he is understood by men of the world. All who have any spark of living faith will understand him in a measure, and the holier he is, they will, for the most part, be attracted the more; but those who serve the world will be blind to him, or scorn and dislike him, the holier he is. This, I say, happened to our Lord. He was All-holy, but "the light shined in darkness, and the darkness comprehended it not." His near relations did not believe in Him. And if this was really so, and for the reason I have said, it surely becomes a question whether we should have understood Him better than they: whether though he had been our next door neighbour, or one of our family, we should have distinguished Him from any one else, who was correct and quiet in his deportment; or rather, whether we should not, though we respected Him, (alas, what a word! what language towards the Most High God!) yet even if we went as far as this, whether we should not have thought Him strange, eccentric, extravagant, and fanciful. Much less should we have detected any sparks of that glory which He had with the Father before the world was, and which was merely hidden not quenched by His earthly tabernacle. This, truly, is a very awful thought; because if He were near us for any long time, and we did not see any thing wonderful in Him, we might take it as a clear proof that we were not His, for "His sheep know His voice, and follow Him;" we might take it as a clear proof that we should not know Him, or admire His greatness, or adore His glory, or love His excellency, if we were admitted to His presence in heaven.

3. And here we are brought to another most serious thought, which I will touch upon. We are very apt to wish we had been born in the days of Christ, and in this way we excuse our misconduct, when conscience reproaches us. We say, that had we had the advantage of being with Christ, we should have had stronger motives, stronger restraints against sin. I answer, that so far from our sinful habits being reformed by the presence of Christ, the chance is, that those same habits would have

hindered us from recognizing Him. We should not have known He was present; and if He had even told us who He was, we should not have believed Him. Nay, had we seen His miracles (incredible as it may seem), even they would not have made any lasting impression on us. Without going into this subject, consider only the possibility of Christ being close to us, even though He did no miracle, and our not knowing it; yet I believe this literally would have been the case with most men. But enough on this subject. What I am coming to is this: I wish you to observe what a fearful light this casts upon our prospects in the next world. We think heaven must be a place of happiness to us, if we do but get there; but the great probability is, if we can judge by what goes on here below, that a bad man, if brought to heaven, would not know He was in heaven;—I do not go to the further question, whether, on the contrary, the very fact of his being in heaven with all his unholiness upon him, would not be a literal torment to him, and light up the fires of hell within him. This indeed would be a most dreadful way of finding out where he was. But let us suppose a lighter case: let us suppose he could remain in heaven unblasted, yet it would seem that at least he would not know that he was there. He would see nothing wonderful there. Could men come nearer to God than when they seized Him, struck Him, spit on Him, hurried Him along, stripped him, stretched out His limbs upon the cross, nailed Him to it, raised it up, stood gazing on Him, jeered Him, gave Him vinegar, looked close whether He was dead, and then pierced Him with a spear? O dreadful thought, that the nearest approaches man has made to God upon earth have been in blasphemy! Whether of the two came closer to Him, St. Thomas, who was allowed to reach forth his hand and reverently touch His wounds, and St. John, who rested on His bosom, or the brutal soldiers who profaned Him limb by limb, and tortured Him nerve by nerve? His Blessed Mother, indeed, came closer still to Him; and we, if we be true believers, still closer, who have Him really, though spiritually, within us; but this is another, an inward sort of approach. Of those who approached Him externally, they came nearest, who knew nothing about it. So it is with sinners: they would walk close to the throne of God; they would stupidly gaze at it; they would touch it; they would meddle with the holiest things; they would go on intruding and prying, not meaning any thing wrong by it, but with a sort of brute curiosity, till the avenging lightnings destroyed them;—all because they have no *senses* to guide them in the matter. Our bodily senses tell us of the approach of good or evil on earth. By sound, by scent, by feeling we know what is happening to us. We know when we are exposing ourselves to the weather, when we are exerting ourselves too much. We have warnings, and feel we must not neglect them. Now, sinners have no spiritual senses; they can presage nothing; they do not know what is going to happen the next moment to them. So they go fearlessly further and further among precipices, till on a sudden they fall, or are smitten and perish. Miserable beings! and this is what sin does for immortal souls; that they should be like the cattle which are slaughtered at the shambles, yet touch and smell the very weapons which are to destroy them!

4. But you may say, how does this concern us? Christ is not here; *we* cannot thus or in any less way insult His Majesty. Are we so sure of this? Certainly we cannot commit such open blasphemy; but it is another matter whether we cannot commit as great. For often sins are greater which are less startling; insults more bitter, which are not so loud; and evils deeper, which are more subtle. Do we not recollect a very awful passage? "Whosoever speaketh a word against the Son of man, it shall be forgiven him; but whosoever speaketh against the Holy Ghost, it shall not be forgiven him."[46] Now, I am not deciding whether or not this denunciation can be fulfilled in the case of Christians now, though when we recollect that we *are* at present under the ministration of that very Spirit of whom our Saviour speaks, this is a very serious question; but I quote it to show that there may be sins greater even than insult and injury offered to Christ's Person, though we should think that impossible, and though they could not be so flagrant or open. With this thought let it be considered:

First, that Christ is still on earth. He said expressly that He would come again. The Holy Ghost's coming is so really His coming, that we might as well say that He was not here in the days of His flesh, when He was visibly in this world, as deny that He is here now, when He is here by His Divine Spirit. This indeed is a mystery, how God the Son and God the Holy Ghost, two Persons, can be one, how He can be in the Spirit and the Spirit in Him; but so it is.

---

46 Matt. 12:32

Next, if He is still on earth, yet is not visible (which cannot be denied), it is plain that He keeps Himself still in the condition which He chose in the days of His flesh. I mean, He is a hidden Saviour, and may be approached (unless we are careful) without due reverence and fear. I say, wherever He is (for that is a further question), still He is here, and again He is secret; and whatever be the tokens of His Presence, still they must be of a nature to admit of persons doubting where it is; and if they will argue, and be sharpwitted and subtle, they may perplex themselves and others, as the Jews did even in the days of His flesh, till He seems to them nowhere present on earth now. And when they come to think him far away, of course they *feel* it to be impossible so to insult Him as the Jews did of old; and if nevertheless He *is* here, they *are* perchance approaching and insulting Him, though they so feel. And this was just the case of the Jews, for they too were ignorant what they were doing. It is probable, then, that we can now commit at least as great blasphemy towards Him as the Jews did first, because we are under the dispensation of that Holy Spirit, against whom even more heinous sins *can* be committed; next, because His presence now as little witnesses of itself, or is impressive to the many, as His bodily presence formerly.

We see a further reason for this apprehension, when we consider what the tokens of His presence now are; for they will be found to be of a nature easily to lead men into irreverence, unless they be humble and watchful. For instance, the Church is called "His Body:" what His material Body was when He was visible on earth, such is the Church now. It is the instrument of His Divine power; it is that which we must approach, to gain good from Him; it is that which by insulting we awaken His anger. Now, what is the Church but, as it were, a body of humiliation, almost provoking insult and profaneness, when men do not live by faith? an earthen vessel, far more so even than His body of flesh, for that was at least pure from all sin, and the Church is defiled in all her members. We know that her ministers at best are but imperfect and erring, and of like passions with their brethren; yet of them He has said, speaking not to the Apostles merely but to all the seventy disciples (to whom Christian ministers are in office surely equal), "He that heareth you, heareth Me, and he that despiseth you, despiseth Me, and he that despiseth Me, despiseth Him that sent Me."

Again: He has made the poor, weak, and afflicted, tokens and instruments of His Presence; and here again, as is plain, the same temptation meets us to neglect or profane it. What He was, such are His chosen followers in this world; and as His obscure and defenceless state led men to insult and ill-treat Him, so the like peculiarities, in the tokens of His Presence, lead men to insult Him now. That such are His tokens is plain from many passages of Scripture: for instance, He says of children, "Whoso shall receive one such little child in My Name, receiveth Me." Again: He said to Saul, who was persecuting His followers, "Why persecutest thou Me?" And He forewarns us, that at the Last Day He will say to the righteous, "I was an hungered, and ye gave Me meat; I was thirsty, and ye gave Me drink; I was a stranger, and ye took Me in;

naked, and ye clothed Me; I was sick, and ye visited Me; I was in prison, and ye came unto Me." And He adds, "Inasmuch as ye have done it unto the least of these My brethren, ye have done it unto Me."[47] He observes the same connexion between Himself and His followers in His words to the wicked. What makes this passage the more awful and apposite, is this, which has been before now remarked, that neither righteous nor wicked *knew* what they had done; even the righteous are represented as unaware that they had approached Christ. They say, "Lord, *when* saw we Thee an hungered, and fed Thee, or thirsty, and gave Thee drink?" In every age, then, Christ is both in the world, and yet not publicly so more than in the days of His flesh.

And a similar remark applies to His Ordinances, which are at once most simple, yet most intimately connected with Him. St. Paul, in his First Epistle to the Corinthians, shows both how easy and how fearful it is to profane the Lord's Supper, while he states how great the excess of the Corinthians had been, yet also that it was a want of "*discerning* the Lord's Body." When He was born into the world, the world knew it not. He was laid in a rude manger, among the cattle, but "all the Angels of God worshipped Him." Now too He is present upon a table, homely perhaps in make, and dishonoured in its circumstances; and faith adores, but the world passes by.

Let us then pray Him ever to enlighten the eyes of our understanding, that we may belong to the Heavenly Host, not to this world. As the carnal-minded would

---

[47] Matt. 18:5.; Acts 9:4; Matt. 25:35-40

not perceive Him even in Heaven, so the spiritual heart may approach Him, possess Him, see Him, even upon earth.

Equanimity

"Rejoice in the Lord alway, and again I say, Rejoice." Phil. 4:4.

In other parts of scripture the prospect of Christ's coming is made a reason for solemn fear and awe, and a call for watching and prayer, but in the verses connected with the text a distinct view of the Christian character is set before us, and distinct duties urged on us. "The Lord is at hand," and what then?—why, if so, we must "rejoice in the Lord;" we must be conspicuous for "moderation;" we must be "careful for nothing;" we must seek from God's bounty, and not from man, whatever we need; we must abound in "thanksgiving;" and we must cherish, or rather we must pray for, and we shall receive from above, "the peace of God which passeth all understanding," to "keep our hearts and minds through Christ Jesus."

Now this is a view of the Christian character definite and complete enough to admit of commenting on,—and it may be useful to show that the thought of Christ's coming not only leads to fear, but to a calm and cheerful frame of mind.

Nothing perhaps is more remarkable than that an Apostle,—a man of toil and blood, a man combating with powers unseen, and a spectacle for men and Angels, and much more that St. Paul, a man whose natural temper was so zealous, so severe, and so vehement,—I say, nothing is more striking and significant than that St. Paul should have given us this view of what a Christian should be. It would be nothing wonderful, it is nothing wonderful, that writers in a day like this should speak of peace, quiet, sobriety, and cheerfulness, as being the tone of mind that becomes a Christian; but considering that St. Paul was by birth a Jew, and by education a Pharisee, that he wrote at a time when, if at any time, Christians were in lively and incessant agitation of mind; when persecution and rumours of persecution abounded; when all things seemed in commotion around them; when there was nothing fixed; when there were no churches to soothe them, no course of worship to sober them, no homes to refresh them; and, again, considering that the Gospel is full of high and noble, and what may be called even romantic, principles and motives, and deep mysteries;—and, further, considering the very topic which the Apostle combines with his admonitions is that awful subject, the coming of Christ;—it is well worthy of notice, that, in such a time, under such a covenant, and with such a prospect, he should draw a picture of the Christian character as free from excitement and effort, as full of repose, as still and as equable, as if the great Apostle wrote in some monastery of the desert or some country parsonage. Here surely is the finger of God; here is the evidence of supernatural influences, making the mind of man independent of circumstances! This is the thought that first suggests itself; and the second is this, how deep and refined is the true Christian spirit!—how difficult to enter into, how vast to embrace, how impossible to exhaust! Who would expect such composure and equanimity from the fervent Apostle of the Gentiles? We know St. Paul could do great things; could suffer and achieve, could preach and confess, could be high and could be low:

but we might have thought that all this was the limit and the perfection of the Christian temper, as he viewed it; and that no room was left him for the feelings which the text and following verses lead us to ascribe to him.

And yet he who "laboured more abundantly than all" his brethren, is also a pattern of simplicity, meekness, cheerfulness, thankfulness, and serenity of mind. These tempers were especially characteristic of St. Paul, and are much insisted on in his Epistles. For instance.—"Mind not high things, but condescend to men of low estate. Be not wise in your own conceits... Provide things honest in the sight of all men. If it be possible, as much as lieth in you, live peaceably with all men." He enjoins, that "the aged men be sober, grave, temperate, sound in faith, in charity, in patience." "The aged women likewise...not false accusers, not given to much wine, teachers of good things, that they may teach the young women to be sober, to love their husbands, to love their children, to be discreet, chaste, keepers at home, good, obedient to their own husbands." And "young men" to be "sober-minded." And it is remarkable that he ends this exhortation with urging the same reason as is given in the verse after the text: "looking for that blessed hope, and the glorious appearing of our great God and Saviour Jesus Christ." In like manner, he says, that Christ's ministers must show "uncorruptness in doctrine, gravity, sincerity, sound speech that cannot be condemned;" that they must be "blameless, not self-willed, not soon angry...

lovers of good men, sober, just, holy, temperate."[48] All this is the description of what seems almost an ordinary character; I mean, it is so staid, so quiet, so unambitious, so homely. It displays so little of what is striking or extraordinary. It is so negligent of this world, so unexcited, so singleminded.

It is observable, too, that it was foretold as the peculiarity of Gospel times by the Prophet Isaiah: "The work of righteousness shall be peace; and the effect of righteousness, quietness and assurance for ever. And My people shall dwell in a peaceable habitation, and in sure dwellings, and in quiet resting-places."[49]

Now then let us consider more particularly what is this state of mind, and what the grounds of it. These seem to be as follows:—The Lord is at hand; this is not your rest; this is not your abiding-place. Act then as persons who are in a dwelling not their own; who are not in their own home; who have not their own goods and furniture about them; who, accordingly, make shift and put up with anything that comes to hand, and do not make a point of things being the best of their kind. "But this I say, brethren, the time is short." What matters it what we eat, what we drink, how we are clothed, where we lodge, what is thought of us, what becomes of us, since we are not at home? It is felt every day, even as regards this world, that when we leave home for a while we are unsettled. This, then, is the kind of feeling which a belief in Christ's coming will create within us. It is not worth while establishing

---

[48] Rom. 12:16-18; Titus 2:2-18; Titus 1:7-8
[49] Isa. 32:17-18

ourselves here; it is not worth while spending time and thought on such an object. We shall hardly have got settled when we shall have to move.

This being apparently the general drift of the passage, let us next enter into the particular portions of it.

1. "Be careful for nothing," he says, or, as St. Peter, "casting all your care upon Him," or, as He Himself, "Take no thought" or care "for the morrow, for the morrow will take thought for the things of itself."[50] This of course is the state of mind which is directly consequent on the belief, that "the Lord is at hand." Who would care for any loss or gain today, if he knew for certain that Christ would show Himself tomorrow? no one. Well, then, the true Christian feels as he would feel, did he know for certain that Christ would be here tomorrow. For he knows for certain, that at least Christ will come to him when he dies; and faith anticipates his death, and makes it just as if that distant day, if it *be* distant, were past and over. One time or another Christ will come, for certain: and when He once *has* come, it matters not what length of time there was before He came;—however long that period may be, it has an end. Judgment is coming, whether it comes sooner or later, and the Christian realizes that it is coming; that is, time does not enter into his calculation, or interfere with his view of things. When men expect to carry out their plans and projects, then they care for them; when they know these will come to nought, they give them over, or become indifferent to them.

---

50 1 Peter 5:7; Matt. 6:34

So, again, it is with all forebodings, anxieties, mortifications, griefs, resentments of this world. "The time is short." It has sometimes been well suggested, as a mode of calming the mind when set upon an object, or much vexed or angered at some occurrence, what will you feel about all this a year hence? It is very plain that matters which agitate us most extremely now, will then interest us not at all; that objects about which we have intense hope and fear now, will then be to us nothing more than things which happen at the other end of the earth. So will it be with all human hopes, fears, pleasures, pains, jealousies, disappointments, successes, when the last day is come. They will have no life in them; they will be as the faded flowers of a banquet, which do but mock us. Or when we lie on the bed of death, what will it avail us to have been rich, or great, or fortunate, or honoured, or influential? All things will then be vanity. Well, what this world will be understood by all to be then, such is it felt to be by the Christian now. He looks at things as he then will look at them, with an uninterested and dispassionate eye, and is neither pained much nor pleased much at the accidents of life, because they are accidents.

2. Another part of the character under review is, what our translation calls moderation; "Let your moderation be known unto all men," or, as it may be more exactly rendered, your consideration, fairness, or equitableness. St. Paul makes it a part of a Christian character to have a reputation for candour, dispassionateness, tenderness towards others. The truth is, as soon and in proportion as a person believes that Christ is coming, and recognises his own position as a

stranger on earth, who has but hired a lodging in it for a season, he will feel indifferent to the course of human affairs. He will be able to look on, instead of taking a part in them. They will be nothing to him. He will be able to criticise them, and pass judgment on them, without partiality. This is what is meant by "our moderation" being acknowledged by all men. Those who have strong interests one way or the other, cannot be dispassionate observers and candid judges. They are partisans; they defend one set of people, and attack another. They are prejudiced against those who differ from them, or who thwart them. They cannot make allowances, or show sympathy for them. But the Christian has no keen expectations, no acute mortifications. He is fair, equitable, considerate towards all men, because he has no temptation to be otherwise. He has no violence, no animosity, no bigotry, no party feeling. He knows that his Lord and Saviour must triumph; he knows that He will one day come from heaven, no one can say how soon. Knowing then the end to which all things tend, he cares less for the road which is to lead to it. When we read a book of fiction, we are much excited with the course of the narrative, till we know how things will turn out; but when we do, the interest ceases. So is it with the Christian. He knows Christ's battle will last till the end; that Christ's cause will triumph in the end; that His Church will last till He comes. He knows what is truth and what is error, where is safety and where is danger; and all this clear knowledge enables him to make concessions, to own difficulties, to do justice to the erring, to acknowledge their good points, to be content with such countenance, greater or less, as he himself receives from others. He does not fear; fear it is that makes men bigots, tyrants, and zealots; but for the Christian, it is his privilege, as he is beyond hopes and fears, suspense and jealousy, so also to be patient, cool, discriminating, and impartial;— so much so, that this very fairness marks his character in the eyes of the world, is "known unto all men."

3. Joy and gladness are also characteristics of him, according to the exhortation in the text, "Rejoice in the Lord alway," and this in spite of the fear and awe which the thought of the Last Day ought to produce in him. It is by means of these strong contrasts that Scripture brings out to us what is the real meaning of its separate portions. If we had been told merely to fear, we should have mistaken a slavish dread, or the gloom of despair, for godly fear; and if we had been told merely to rejoice, we should perhaps have mistaken a rude freedom and familiarity for joy; but when we are told both to fear and to rejoice, we gain thus much at first sight, that our joy is not to be irreverent, nor our fear to be desponding; that though both feelings are to remain, neither is to be what it would be by itself. This is what we gain at once by such contrasts. I do not say that this makes it at all easier to combine the separate duties to which they relate; that is a further and higher work; but thus much we gain at once, a better knowledge of those separate duties themselves. And now I am speaking about the duty of rejoicing, and I say, that whatever be the duty of fearing greatly and trembling greatly at the thought of the Day of Judgment, and of course it is a great duty, yet the command so to do cannot reverse the command to rejoice; it can only so far interfere with

it as to explain what is meant by rejoicing. It is as clear a duty to rejoice in the prospect of Christ's coming, as if we were not told to fear it. The duty of fearing does but perfect our joy; that joy alone is true Christian joy, which is informed and quickened by fear, and made thereby sober and reverent.

How joy and fear can be reconciled, words cannot show. Act and deed alone can show how. Let a man try both to fear and to rejoice, as Christ and His Apostles tell him, and in time he will learn how; but when he has learned, he will be as little able to explain how it is he does both, as he was before. He will seem inconsistent, and may easily be proved to be so, to the satisfaction of irreligious men, as Scripture is called inconsistent. He becomes the paradox which Scripture enjoins. This is variously fulfilled in the case of men of advanced holiness. They are accused of the most opposite faults; of being proud, and of being mean; of being over-simple, and being crafty; of having too strict, and, at the same time, too lax a conscience; of being unsocial, and yet being worldly; of being too literal in explaining Scripture, and yet of adding to Scripture, and superseding Scripture. Men of the world or men of inferior religiousness, cannot understand them, and are fond of criticising those who, in seeming to be inconsistent, are but like Scripture teaching.

But to return to the case of joy and fear. It may be objected, that at least those who fall into sin, or who have in times past sinned grievously, cannot have this pleasant and cheerful temper which St. Paul enjoins. I grant it. But what is this but saying that St. Paul enjoins us *not* to fall into sin? When St. Paul warns us against sadness and heaviness, of course he warns us against those things which make men sad and heavy; and therefore especially against sin, which is an especial enemy of joyfulness. It is not that sorrowing for sin is wrong when we *have* sinned, but the *sinning* is wrong which causes the sorrowing. When a person has sinned, he cannot do anything better than sorrow. He ought to sorrow; and so far as he does sorrow, he is certainly *not* in the perfect Christian state; but it is his sin that has forfeited it. And yet even here sorrow is not inconsistent with rejoicing. For there are few men, who are really in earnest in their sorrow, but after a time may be conscious that they are so; and, when man knows himself to be in earnest, he knows that God looks mercifully upon him; and this gives him sufficient reason for rejoicing, even though fear remains. St. Peter could appeal to Christ, "Lord, Thou knowest all things; Thou knowest that I love Thee." We of course cannot appeal so unreservedly—still we can timidly appeal— we can say that we humbly trust that, whatever be the measure of our past sins, and whatever of our present self-denial, yet at bottom we do wish and strive to give up the world and to follow Christ; and in proportion as this sense of sincerity is strong upon our minds, in the same degree shall we rejoice in the Lord, even while we fear.

4. Once more, peace is part of this same temper also. "The peace of God," says the Apostle, "which passeth all understanding, shall keep your hearts and minds through Christ Jesus." There are many things in the Gospel to alarm us, many to agitate us, many to

transport us, but the end and issue of all these is *peace*. "Glory to God in the highest, and on earth peace." It may be asked indeed whether warfare, perplexity, and uncertainty be not the condition of the Christian here below; whether St. Paul himself does not say that he has "the care," or the anxiety, "of all the Churches," and whether he does not plainly evince and avow in his Epistles to the Galatians and Corinthians much distress of mind? "Without were fightings, within fears."[51] I grant it; he certainly shows at times much agitation of mind; but consider this. Did you ever look at an expanse of water, and observe the ripples on the surface? Do you think that disturbance penetrates below it? Nay; you have seen or heard of fearful tempests on the sea; scenes of horror and distress, which are in no respect a fit type of an Apostle's tears or sighings about his flock. Yet even these violent commotions do not reach into the depths. The foundations of the ocean, the vast realms of water which girdle the earth, are as tranquil and as silent in the storm as in a calm. So is it with the souls of holy men. They have a well of peace springing up within them unfathomable; and though the accidents of the hour may make them seem agitated, yet in their hearts they are not so. Even Angels joy over sinners repentant, and, as we may therefore suppose, grieve over sinners impenitent,—yet who shall say that they have not perfect peace? Even Almighty God Himself deigns to speak of His being grieved, and angry, and rejoicing,— yet is He not the unchangeable? And in like manner, to

---

[51] 2 Cor. 7:5

compare human things with divine, St. Paul had perfect peace, as being stayed in soul on God, though the trials of life might vex him.

For, as I have said, the Christian has a deep, silent, hidden peace, which the world sees not,—like some well in a retired and shady place, difficult of access. He is the greater part of his time by himself, and when he is in solitude, that is his real state. What he is when left to himself and to his God, that is his true life. He can bear himself; he can (as it were) joy in himself, for it is the grace of God within him, it is the presence of the Eternal Comforter, in which he joys. He can bear, he finds it pleasant, to be with himself at all times, —"never less alone than when alone." He can lay his head on his pillow at night, and own in God's sight, with overflowing heart, that he wants nothing,—that he "is full and abounds,"—that God has been all things to him, and that nothing is not his which God could give him. More thankfulness, more holiness, more of heaven he needs indeed, but the thought that he can have more is not a thought of trouble, but of joy. It does not interfere with his peace to know that he may grow nearer God. Such is the Christian's peace, when, with a single heart and the Cross in his eye, he addresses and commends himself to Him with whom the night is as clear as the day. St. Paul says that "the peace of God shall *keep* our hearts and minds." By "keep" is meant "guard," or "garrison," our hearts; so as to keep out enemies. And he says, our "hearts and minds" in contrast to what the world sees of us. Many hard things may be said of the Christian, and done against him, but he has a secret preservative or charm, and minds them not.

These are some few suggestions on that character of mind which becomes the followers of Him who was once "born of a pure Virgin," and who bids them as "newborn babes desire the sincere milk of the Word, that they may grow thereby." The Christian is cheerful, easy, kind, gentle, courteous, candid, unassuming; has no pretence, no affectation, no ambition, no singularity; because he has neither hope nor fear about this world. He is serious, sober, discreet, grave, moderate, mild, with so little that is unusual or striking in his bearing, that he may easily be taken at first sight for an ordinary man. There are persons who think religion consists in ecstasies, or in set speeches;—he is not of those. And it must be confessed, on the other hand, that there is a common-place state of mind which does show itself calm, composed, and candid, yet is very far from the true Christian temper. In this day especially it is very easy for men to be benevolent, liberal, and dispassionate. It costs nothing to be dispassionate when you feel nothing, to be cheerful when you have nothing to fear, to be generous or liberal when what you give is not your own, and to be benevolent and considerate when you have no principles and no opinions. Men nowadays are moderate and equitable, not because the Lord is at hand, but because they do not feel that He is coming. Quietness is a grace, not in itself, only when it is grafted on the stem of faith, zeal, self-abasement, and diligence.

May it be our blessedness, as years go on, to add one grace to another, and advance upward, step by step, neither neglecting the lower after attaining the higher, nor aiming at the higher before attaining the lower. The first grace is faith, the last is love; first comes zeal, afterwards comes loving-kindness; first comes humiliation, then comes peace; first comes diligence, then comes resignation. May we learn to mature all graces in us;—fearing and trembling, watching and repenting, because Christ is coming; joyful, thankful, and careless of the future, because He is come.

Remembrance of Past Mercies

"I am not worthy of the least of all the mercies, and of all the truth, which Thou hast showed unto Thy servant." Gen. 32:10.

The spirit of humble thankfulness for past mercies which these words imply, is a grace to which we are especially called in the Gospel. Jacob, who spoke them, knew not of those great and wonderful acts of love with which God has since visited the race of man. But though he might not know the depths of God's counsels, he knew himself so far as to know that he was worthy of no good thing at all, and he knew also that Almighty God had shown him great mercies and great truth: mercies, in that He had done for him good things, whereas he had deserved evil; and truth, in that He had made him promises, and had been faithful to them. In consequence, he overflowed with gratitude when he looked back upon the past; marvelling at the contrast between what he was in himself and what God had been to him.

Such thankfulness, I say, is eminently a Christian grace, and is enjoined on us in the New Testament. For instance, we are exhorted to be "thankful," and to let "the Word of Christ dwell in us richly in all wisdom; teaching and admonishing one another in psalms and hymns and spiritual songs, singing with grace in our hearts to the Lord."

Elsewhere, we are told to "speak to ourselves in psalms and hymns and spiritual songs, singing and making melody in our heart to the Lord: giving thanks always for all things unto God and the Father, in the Name of our Lord Jesus Christ."

Again: "Be careful for nothing: but in every thing by prayer and supplication, with thanksgiving, let your requests be made known unto God."

Again: "In every thing give thanks: for this is the will of God in Christ Jesus concerning you."[52]

The Apostle, who writes all this, was himself an especial pattern of a thankful spirit: "Rejoice in the Lord alway," he says: "and again I say, Rejoice." I have learned, in whatsoever state I am, therewith to be content. I have all and abound; I am full." Again: "I thank Christ Jesus our Lord, who hath enabled me, for that He counted me faithful, putting me into the ministry; who was before a blasphemer and a persecutor, and injurious. But I obtained mercy, because I did it ignorantly in unbelief. And the grace of our Lord was exceeding abundant, with faith and love which is in Christ Jesus."[53] O great Apostle! how could it be otherwise, considering what he had been and what he was,—transformed from an enemy to a friend, from a blind Pharisee to an inspired preacher? And yet there is another Saint, besides the patriarch Jacob, who is his fellow in this excellent grace,—like them, distinguished by great vicissitudes of life, and by the adoring love and the tenderness of heart with which he looked back upon the past:—I mean, "David, the son of Jesse, the

---

52 Col. 3:15-16; Eph. 5:19-20; Phil. 4:6; 1 Thess. 5:18
53 Phil. 4:4, 11, 18; 1 Tim. 1:12-14

man who was raised up on high, the anointed of the God of Jacob, and the sweet Psalmist of Israel."[54]

The Book of Psalms is full of instances of David's thankful spirit, which I need not cite here, as we are all so well acquainted with them. I will but refer to his thanksgiving, when he set apart the precious materials for the building of the Temple, as it occurs at the end of the First Book of Chronicles; when he rejoiced so greatly, because he and his people had the heart to offer freely to God, and thanked God for his very thankfulness. "David, the king...rejoiced with great joy; wherefore David blessed the Lord before all the congregation; and David said, Blessed be Thou, Lord God of Israel, our Father, for ever and ever... Both riches and honour come of Thee, and Thou reignest over all; and in Thine hand is power and might, and in Thine hand it is to make great, and to give strength unto all. Now, therefore, our God, we thank Thee, and praise Thy glorious Name. But who am I, and what is my people, that we should be able to offer so willingly after this sort? for all things come of Thee, and of Thine own have we given Thee."[55]

Such was the thankful spirit of David, looking back upon the past, wondering and rejoicing at the way in which his Almighty Protector had led him on, and at the works He had enabled him to do; and praising and glorifying Him for His mercy and truth. David, then, Jacob, and St. Paul, may be considered the three great patterns of thankfulness, which are set before us in

---

[54] 2 Sam. 23:1
[55] 1 Chron. 29:9-14

Scripture;—saints, all of whom were peculiarly the creation of God's grace, and whose very life and breath it was humbly and adoringly to meditate upon the contrast between what, in different ways, they had been, and what they were. A perishing wanderer had unexpectedly become a patriarch; a shepherd, a king; and a persecutor, an apostle: each had been chosen, at God's inscrutable pleasure, to fulfil a great purpose, and each, while he did his utmost to fulfil it, kept praising God that he was made His instrument. Of the first, it was said, "Jacob have I loved, but Esau have I hated;" of the second, that "He refused the tabernacle of Joseph, and chose not the tribe of Ephraim, but chose the tribe of Judah, even the hill of Sion, which He loved: He chose David also His servant, and took him away from the sheepfolds." And St. Paul says of himself, "Last of all, He was seen of me also, as of one born out of due time."[56]

These thoughts naturally come over the mind at this season, when we are engaged in celebrating God's grace in making us His children, by the incarnation of His Only-begotten Son, the greatest and most wonderful of all His mercies. And to the Patriarch Jacob our minds are now particularly turned, by the First Lessons for this day, taken from the Prophet Isaiah, in which the Church is addressed and comforted under the name of Jacob. Let us then, in this season of thankfulness, and at the beginning of a new year, take a brief view of the character of this Patriarch; and though David and Isaiah be the prophets of grace, and St. Paul its special

---

[56] Rom. 9:13; Ps. 78:68-71; 1 Cor. 15:8

herald and chief pattern, yet, if we wish to see an actual specimen of a habit of thankfulness occupied in the remembrance of God's mercies, I think we shall not be wrong in betaking ourselves to Jacob.

Jacob's distinguishing grace then, as I think it may be called, was a habit of affectionate musing upon God's providences towards him in times past, and of overflowing thankfulness for them. Not that he had not other graces also, but this seems to have been his distinguishing grace. All good men have in their measure all graces; for He, by whom they have any, does not give one apart from the whole: He gives the root, and the root puts forth branches. But since time, and circumstances, and their own use of the gift, and their own disposition and character, have much influence on the mode of its manifestation, so it happens, that each good man has his own distinguishing grace, apart from the rest, his own particular hue and fragrance and fashion, as a flower may have. As, then, there are numberless flowers on the earth, all of them flowers, and so far like each other; and all springing from the same earth, and nourished by the same air and dew, and none without beauty; and yet some are more beautiful than others; and of those which are beautiful, some excel in colour and others in sweetness, and others in form; and then, again, those which are sweet have such perfect sweetness, yet so distinct, that we do not know how to compare them together, or to say which is the sweeter: so is it with souls filled and nurtured by God's secret grace. Abraham, for instance, Jacob's forefather, was the pattern of faith. This is insisted on in Scripture, and it is not here necessary to show that he was so. It will be sufficient to say, that he left his country at God's word; and, at the same word, took up the knife to slay his own son. Abraham seems to have had something very noble and magnanimous about him. He could realize and make present to him things unseen. He followed God in the dark as promptly, as firmly, with as cheerful a heart, and bold a stepping, as if he were in broad daylight. There is something very great in this; and, therefore, St. Paul calls Abraham *our* father, the father of Christians as well as of Jews. For we are especially bound to walk by faith, not by sight; and are blessed in faith, and justified by faith, as was faithful Abraham. Now (if I may say it, with due reverence to the memory of that favoured servant of God, in whose praise I am now speaking) that faith in which Abraham excelled was not Jacob's characteristic excellence. Not that he had not faith, and great faith, else he would not have been so dear to God. His buying the birthright and gaining the blessing from Esau were proofs of faith. Esau saw nothing or little precious in them,—he was profane; easily parted with the one, and had no high ideas of the other. However, Jacob's faith, earnest and vigorous as it was, was not like Abraham's. Abraham kept his affections loose from everything earthly, and was ready, at God's word, to slay his only son. Jacob had many sons, and may we not even say that he indulged them overmuch? Even as regards Joseph, whom he so deservedly loved, beautiful and touching as his love of him is, yet there is a great contrast between his feelings towards the "son of his old age" and those of Abraham towards Isaac, the unexpected offspring of his hundredth year,—nor only such, but his long-promised only son, with whom were the promises. Again: Abraham left his country,—so did Jacob; but Abraham, at God's word,—Jacob, from necessity on the threat of Esau. Abraham, from the first, felt that God was his portion and his inheritance, and, in a great and generous spirit, he freely gave up all he had, being sure that he should find what was more excellent in doing so. But Jacob, in spite of his really living by faith, wished (if we may so say), as one passage of his history shows, to see before he fully believed. When he was escaping from Esau and came to Bethel, and God appeared to him in a dream and gave him promises, but not yet the performance of them,—what did he do? Did he simply accept them? He says, "*If* God will be with me, and will keep me in this way that I go, and will give me bread to eat, and raiment to put on, so that I come again to my father's house in peace, *then* shall the Lord be my God."[57] He makes his obedience, in some sense, depend on a condition; and although we must not, and need not, take the words as if he meant that he would not serve God *till* and *unless* He did for him what He had promised, yet they seem to show a fear and anxiety, gentle indeed, and subdued, and very human (and therefore the more interesting and winning in the eyes of us common men, who read his words), yet an anxiety which Abraham had not. We feel Jacob to be more like ourselves than Abraham was.

What, then, was Jacob's distinguishing grace, as faith was Abraham's? I have already said it: I suppose,

---

[57] Gen. 28:20-21

thankfulness. Abraham appears ever to have been looking forward in *hope*,—Jacob looking back in *memory*: the one rejoicing in the future, the other in the past; the one setting his affections on the future, the other on the past; the one making his way towards the promises, the other musing over their fulfilment. Not that Abraham did not look back also, and Jacob, as he says on his death-bed, did not "wait for the salvation" of God; but this was the difference between them, Abraham was a hero, Jacob "a plain man, dwelling in tents."

Jacob seems to have had a gentle, tender, affectionate, timid mind—easily frightened, easily agitated, loving God so much that he feared to lose Him, and, like St. Thomas perhaps, anxious for sight and possession from earnest and longing desire of them. Were it not for faith, love would become impatient, and thus Jacob desired to possess, not from cold incredulity or hardness of heart, but from such a loving impatience. Such men are easily downcast, and must be treated kindly; they soon despond, they shrink from the world, for they feel its rudeness, which bolder natures do not. Neither Abraham nor Jacob loved the world. But Abraham did not fear, did not feel it. Jacob felt and winced, as being wounded by it. You recollect his touching complaints, "All these things are against me!"—"Then shall ye bring down my grey hairs with sorrow to the grave."—"If I am bereaved of my children, I am bereaved." Again, elsewhere we are told, "All his sons and all his daughters rose up to comfort him, but he refused to be comforted." At another time, "Jacob's heart fainted, for he believed them not." Again,

"The spirit of Jacob their father revived."[58] You see what a childlike, sensitive, sweet mind he had. Accordingly, as I have said, his happiness lay, not in looking forward to the hope, but backwards upon the experience, of God's mercies towards him. He delighted lovingly to trace, and gratefully to acknowledge, what had been given, leaving the future to itself.

For instance, when coming to meet Esau, he brings before God in prayer, in words of which the text is part, what He had already done for him, recounting His past favours with great and humble joy in the midst of his present anxiety. "O God of my father Abraham," he says, "and God of my father Isaac, the Lord which saidst unto me, Return unto thy country, and to thy kindred, and I will deal well with thee: I am not worthy of the least of all the mercies, and of all the truth, *which Thou hast showed unto Thy servant; for with my staff I passed over this Jordan, and now I am become two bands.*" Again, after he had returned to his own land, he proceeded to fulfil the promise he had made to consecrate Bethel as a house of God, "Let us arise, and go up to Bethel; and I will make there an altar unto God, *who answered me in the day of my distress, and was with me in the way which I went.*" Again, to Pharaoh, still dwelling on the past: "The days of the years of my pilgrimage are an hundred and thirty years; few and evil have the days of the years of my life been," he means, in themselves, and as separate from God's favour, "and have not attained unto the days of the years of the life of my fathers, in the days of their

<hr>

[58] Gen. 62:36, 38; Gen. 43:14; Gen. 37:35, 45:26-27

pilgrimage." Again, when he was approaching his end, he says to Joseph, "God Almighty *appeared unto me* at Luz," that is, Bethel, "in the land of Canaan, and blessed me." Again, still looking back, "As for me, when I came from Padan, Rachel died by me in the land of Canaan, in the way, when yet there was but a little way to come to Ephrath; and I buried her there in the way of Ephrath." Again, his blessing upon Ephraim and Manasseh: "God, before whom my fathers Abraham and Isaac did walk, *the God which fed me all my life long unto this day*, the Angel which redeemed me from all evil, bless the lads." Again he looks back on the land of promise, though in the plentifulness of Egypt: "Behold, I die, but God shall be with you, and bring you again unto the land of your fathers." And when he gives command about his burial, he says: "I am to be gathered unto my people; bury me with my fathers in the cave that is in the field of Ephron the Hittite." He gives orders to be buried with his fathers; this was natural, but observe, he goes on to *enlarge* on the subject, after his special manner: "There they buried Abraham and Sarah his wife; there they buried Isaac and Rebekah his wife; and *there I buried Leah*." And further on, when he speaks of waiting for God's salvation, which is an act of hope, he so words it as at the same time to dwell upon the past: "I *have* waited," he says, that is, all my life long, "I have waited for Thy salvation, O Lord."[59] Such was Jacob, living in memory rather than in hope, counting times, recording seasons, keeping days; having his history by heart, and his past

---

[59] Gen. 32:9-10; 35:3; 47:9; 48:3, 7, 15, 16, 21; 49:29-31; Gen. 49:18

life in his hand; and as if to carry on his mind into that of his descendants, it was enjoined upon them, that once a year every Israelite should appear before God with a basket of fruit of the earth, and call to mind what God had done for him and his father Jacob, and express his thankfulness for it. "A Syrian ready to perish was my father," he had to say, meaning Jacob; "and he went down into Egypt, and sojourned there, and became a nation, great, mighty, and populous ... And the Lord brought us forth out of Egypt with an outstretched arm, and with great terribleness, and with signs, and with wonders; and hath brought us into this land…that floweth with milk and honey. And now, behold, I have brought the first-fruits of the land, which Thou, O Lord, hast given me."[60]

Well were it for us, if we had the character of mind instanced in Jacob, and enjoined on his descendants; the temper of dependence upon God's providence, and thankfulness under it, and careful memory of all He has done for us. It would be well if we were in the habit of looking at all we have as God's gift, undeservedly given, and day by day continued to us solely by His mercy. He gave; He may take away. He gave us all we have, life, health, strength, reason, enjoyment, the light of conscience; whatever we have good and holy within us; whatever faith we have; whatever of a renewed will; whatever love towards Him; whatever power over ourselves; whatever prospect of heaven. He gave us relatives, friends, education, training, knowledge, the Bible, the Church. All comes from Him. He gave; He

[60] Deut. 36:5-10

135

may take away. Did He take away, we should be called on to follow Job's pattern, and be resigned: "The Lord gave, and the Lord hath taken away. Blessed be the Name of the Lord."[61] While He continues His blessings, we should follow David and Jacob, by living in constant praise and thanksgiving, and in offering up to Him of His own.

We are not our own, any more than what we possess is our own. We did not make ourselves; we cannot be supreme over ourselves. We cannot be our own masters. We are God's property by creation, by redemption, by regeneration. He has a triple claim upon us. Is it not our happiness thus to view the matter? Is it any happiness, or any comfort, to consider that we *are* our own? It may be thought so by the young and prosperous. These may think it a great thing to have everything, as they suppose, their own way,—to depend on no one,—to have to think of nothing out of sight,—to be without the irksomeness of continual acknowledgment, continual prayer, continual reference of what they do to the will of another. But as time goes on, they, as all men, will find that independence was not made for man —that it is an unnatural state—may do for a while, but will not carry us on safely to the end. No, we are creatures; and, as being such, we have two duties, to be resigned and to be thankful.

Let us then view God's providences towards us more religiously than we have hitherto done. Let us try to gain a truer view of what we are, and where we are, in His kingdom. Let us humbly and reverently attempt to

---

[61] Job 1:21

trace His guiding hand in the years which we have hitherto lived. Let us thankfully commemorate the many mercies He has vouchsafed to us in time past, the many sins He has not remembered, the many dangers He has averted, the many prayers He has answered, the many mistakes He has corrected, the many warnings, the many lessons, the much light, the abounding comfort which He has from time to time given. Let us dwell upon times and seasons, times of trouble, times of joy, times of trial, times of refreshment. How did He cherish us as children! How did He guide us in that dangerous time when the mind began to think for itself, and the heart to open to the world! How did He with his sweet discipline restrain our passions, mortify our hopes, calm our fears, enliven our heavinesses, sweeten our desolateness, and strengthen our infirmities! How did He gently guide us towards the strait gate! how did He allure us along His everlasting way, in spite of its strictness, in spite of its loneliness, in spite of the dim twilight in which it lay! He has been all things to us. He has been, as He was to Abraham, Isaac, and Jacob, our God, our shield, and great reward, promising and performing, day by day. "Hitherto hath He helped us." "He hath been mindful of us, and He will bless us." He has not made us for nought; He has brought us thus far, in order to bring us further, in order to bring us on to the end. He will never leave us nor forsake us; so that we may boldly say, "The Lord is my Helper; I will not fear what flesh can do unto me." We may "cast all our care upon Him, who careth for us." What is it to us how our future path lies, if it be but His path? What is it to us whither it leads us, so that in the end it leads to

Him? What is it to us what He puts upon us, so that He enables us to undergo it with a pure conscience, a true heart, not desiring anything of this world in comparison of Him? What is it to us what terror befalls us, if He be but at hand to protect and strengthen us? "Thou, Israel," He says, "art My servant Jacob, whom I have chosen, the seed of Abraham My friend." "Fear not thou worm Jacob, and ye men of Israel; I will help thee, saith the Lord, and thy Redeemer, the Holy One of Israel." "Thus saith the Lord that created thee, O Jacob, and He that formed thee, O Israel, Fear not; for I have redeemed thee, I have called thee by thy name; thou art Mine. When thou passest through the waters, I will be with thee; and through the rivers, they shall not overflow thee; when thou walkest through the fire, thou shalt not be burned; neither shall the flame kindle upon thee. For I am the Lord thy God, the Holy One of Israel, thy Saviour."[62]

---

[62] Isa. 41:8, 14; 43:1-3

The Mystery of Godliness

"Both He that sanctifieth and they who are sanctified are all of one: for which cause He is not ashamed to call them brethren."
Heb. 2:11.

Our Saviour's birth in the flesh is an earnest, and, as it were, beginning of our birth in the Spirit. It is a figure, promise, or pledge of our new birth, and it effects what it promises. As He was born, so are we born also; and since He was born, therefore we too are born. As He is the Son of God by nature, so are we sons of God by grace; and it is He who has made us such. This is what the text says; He is the "Sanctifier," we the "sanctified." Moreover, He and we, says the text, "are all of one." God sanctifies the Angels, but there the Creator and the creature are not of one. But the Son of God and we are of one; He has become "the firstborn of every creature;" He has taken our nature, and in and through it He sanctifies us. He is our brother by virtue of His incarnation, and, as the text says, "He is not ashamed to call us brethren;" and, having sanctified our nature in Himself, He communicates it to us.

1. This is the wonderful economy of grace, or mystery of godliness, which should be before our minds at all times, but especially at this season, when the Most Holy took upon Him our flesh of "a pure Virgin," "by the operation of the Holy Ghost, without spot of sin, to make us clean from all sin." God "dwelleth in the Light which no man can approach

unto;" He "is Light, and in Him is no darkness at all." "His garment," as described in the Prophet's Vision, is "white as snow, and the hair of His head like the pure wool; His throne the fiery flame, and His wheels burning fire." And in like manner the Son of God, because He is the Son, is light also. He is "the True Light, which lighteth every man that cometh into the world." On His transfiguration "His face did shine as the sun," and "His raiment became shining, exceeding white as snow," "white and glistering." And when He appeared to St. John, "His head and His hairs were white like wool, as white as snow; and His eyes were as a flame of fire: and His feet like unto fine brass, as if they burnt in a furnace; and His countenance was as the sun shineth in his strength."[63] Such was our Lord's holiness because He was the Son of God from eternity. There was always the Father, always the Son: always the Father, *therefore* always the Son, for the Name of Father implies the Son, and never was there a time when the Father Almighty was not, and in the Father the Son also. He it is who is spoken of in the beginning of St. John's Gospel, when it is said, "In the beginning was the Word, and the Word was with God, and the Word was God." Soon after, the same Apostle speaks of Him as "in the bosom of the Father." And He speaks Himself of "the glory which He had with the Father before the world was." And St. Paul calls Him "the Brightness of God's glory, and the express Image of His Person." And elsewhere, "the Image of the Invisible God." Thus what our Lord is, that none other

---

[63] 1 Tim. 6:16; 1 John 1:5.; Dan. 7:9; John 1:9; Matt. 17:2; Mark 9:3; Luke 11:29; Rev. 1:14-16

can be; He is the Only-begotten Son; He has the Divine nature, and is of one substance with the Father, which cannot be said of any creature. He is one with God, and His nature is secret and incommunicable. Hence St. Paul contrasts His dignity with that of Angels, the highest of all creatures, with a view of showing the infinite superiority of the Son. "Unto which of the Angels said He at any time, Thou art My Son, this day have I begotten Thee?" Again, "When He bringeth in the first-begotten into the world, He saith, And let all the Angels of God worship Him." And again, "To which of the Angels saith He at any time, Sit on My right hand until I make Thine enemies Thy footstool?" Of the Angels we are told, "He putteth no trust in His saints; yea, the heavens are not clean in His sight;" but our Lord is His "beloved Son, in whom He is well pleased."[64]

He it was who created the worlds; He it was who interposed of old time in the affairs of the world, and showed Himself to be a living and observant God, whether men thought of Him or not. Yet this great God condescended to come down on earth from His heavenly throne, and to be born into His own world; showing Himself as the Son of God in a new and second sense, in a created nature, as well as in His eternal substance. Such is the first reflection which the birth of Christ suggests.

2. And next, observe, that since He was the All-holy Son of God, though He condescended to be born into the world, He necessarily came into it in a way suitable

---

[64] John 1:1; 17:5; Heb. 1:5, *et seq.*; Col. 1:15; Job 15:15; Matt. 3:17

to the All-holy, and different from that of other men. He took our nature upon Him, but not our sin; taking our nature in a way above nature. Did He then come from heaven in the clouds? did He frame a body for Himself out of the dust of the earth? No; He was, as other men, "made of a woman," as St. Paul speaks, that He might take on Him, not another nature, but the nature of man. It had been prophesied from the beginning, that the Seed of the woman should bruise the serpent's head. "I will put enmity," said Almighty God to the serpent at the fall, "between thee and the woman, and between thy seed and her Seed; It shall bruise thy head."[65] In consequence of this promise, pious women, we are told, were in the old time ever looking out in hope that in their own instance per-adventure the promise might find its accomplishment. One after another hoped in turn that she herself might be mother of the promised King; and therefore marriage was in repute, and virginity in disesteem, as if then only they had a prospect of being the Mother of Christ, if they waited for the blessing according to the course of nature, and amid the generations of men. Pious women they were, but little comprehending the real condition of mankind. It was ordained, indeed, that the Eternal Word should come into the world by the ministration of a woman; but born in the way of the flesh He could not be. Mankind is a fallen race; ever since the Fall there has been a "fault and corruption of the nature of every man that naturally is engendered of the offspring of Adam...so that the flesh lusteth always

---

[65] Gen. 3:15

contrary to the Spirit, and therefore in every person born into this world it deserveth God's wrath and damnation." And "the Apostle doth confess that concupiscence and lust hath of itself the nature of sin." "That which is born of the flesh, is flesh." "Who can bring a clean thing out of an unclean?" "How can he be clean that is born of a woman?" Or as holy David cries out, "Behold, I was shapen in wickedness, and in sin hath my mother conceived me."[66] No one is born into the world without sin; or can rid himself of the sin of his birth except by a second birth through the Spirit. How then could the Son of God have come as a Holy Saviour, had He come as other men? How could He have atoned for our sins, who Himself had guilt? or cleansed our hearts, who was impure Himself? or raised up our heads, who was Himself the son of shame? Surely any such messenger had needed a Saviour for his own disease, and to such a one would apply the proverb, "Physician, heal thyself." Priests among men are they who have to offer "first for their own sins, and then for the people's;"[67] but He, coming as the immaculate Lamb of God, and the all-prevailing Priest, could not come in the way which those fond persons anticipated. He came by a new and living way, by which He alone has come, and which alone became Him. The Prophet Isaiah had been the first to announce it: "The Lord Himself shall give you a sign," he says, "Behold, a Virgin shall conceive and bear a Son, and shall call His Name Immanuel." And accordingly St. Matthew after quoting this text, declares its fulfilment in the instance

---

[66] John 3:6; Job 14:4; 25:4; Ps. 51:5
[67] Heb. 7:27

of the Blessed Mary. "All this," he says, "was done that it might be fulfilled which was spoken by the prophet." And further, two separate Angels, one to Mary, one to Joseph, declare who the adorable Agent was, by whom this miracle was wrought. "Joseph, thou son of David," an Angel said to him, "fear not to take unto thee Mary thy wife, for that which is conceived in her is of the Holy Ghost;" and what followed from this? He proceeds, "And she shall bring forth a Son, and thou shalt call His Name Jesus, for He shall save His people from their sins." Because He was "incarnate by the Holy Ghost of the Virgin Mary," therefore He was "Jesus," a "Saviour from sin." Again, the Angel Gabriel had already said to Mary, "Hail, thou that art highly favoured, the Lord is with thee: blessed art thou among women." And then he proceeds to declare, that her Son should be called Jesus; that He "should be great, and should be called the Son of the Highest;" and that "of His Kingdom there shall be no end." And he concludes by announcing, "The Holy Ghost shall come upon thee, and the power of the Highest shall overshadow thee; therefore that Holy Thing which shall be born of thee shall be called the Son of God."[68] Because God the Holy Ghost wrought miraculously, therefore was her Son a "Holy Thing," "the Son of God," and "Jesus," and the heir of an everlasting kingdom.

3. This is the great Mystery which we are now celebrating, of which mercy is the beginning, and sanctity the end: according to the Psalm, "Righteousness and peace have kissed each other." He

---

[68] Matt. 1:20-21; Luke 1:28-35

who is all purity came to an impure race to raise them to His purity. He, the brightness of God's glory, came in a body of flesh, which was pure and holy as Himself, "without spot, or wrinkle, or any such thing, but holy and without blemish;" and this He did for our sake, "that we might be partakers of His holiness." He needed not a human nature for Himself,—He was all-perfect in His original Divine nature; but He took upon Himself what was ours for the sake of us. He who "hath made of one blood all nations of men," so that in the sin of one all sinned, and in the death of one all died, He came in that very nature of Adam, in order to communicate to us that nature as it is in His Person, that "our sinful bodies might be made clean by His Body, and our souls washed through His most precious Blood;" to make us partakers of the Divine nature; to sow the seed of eternal life in our hearts; and to raise us from "the corruption that is in the world through lust," to that immaculate purity and that fulness of grace which is in Him. He who is the first principle and pattern of all things, came to be the beginning and pattern of human kind, the firstborn of the whole creation. He, who is the everlasting Light, became the Light of men; He, who is the Life from eternity, became the Life of a race dead in sin; He, who is the Word of God, came to be a spiritual Word, "dwelling richly in our hearts," an "engrafted Word, which is able to save our souls;" He, who is the co-equal Son of the Father, came to be the Son of God in our flesh, that He might raise us also to the adoption of sons, and might be first among many brethren. And this is the reason why the Collect for the season, after speaking of our Lord as the Only-begotten Son, and born in our nature of a pure Virgin, proceeds to speak of our new birth and adopted sonship, and renewal by the grace of the Holy Ghost.

4. And when He came into the world, He was a pattern of sanctity in the circumstances of his life, as well as in His birth. He did not implicate and contaminate Himself with sinners. He came down from heaven, and made a short work in righteousness, and then returned back again where He was before. He came into the world, and He speedily left the world; as if to teach us how little He Himself, how little we His followers, have to do with the world. He, the Eternal Ever-living Word of God, did not outlive Methuselah's years, nay, did not even exhaust the common age of man; but He came and He went, before men knew that He had come, like the lightning shining from one side of heaven unto the other, as being the beginning of a new and invisible creation, and having no part in the old Adam. He was in the world, but not of the world; and while He was here, He, the Son of man, was still in heaven: and as well might fire feed upon water, or the wind be subjected to man's bidding, as the Only-begotten Son really be portion and member of that perishable system in which He condescended to move. He could not rest or tarry upon earth; He did but do His work in it; He could but come and go.

And while He was here, since He could not acquiesce or pleasure Himself in the earth, so He would none of its vaunted goods. When He humbled himself unto His own sinful creation, He would not let that creation minister to Him of its best, as if disdaining to receive offering or tribute from a fallen world. It is only nature regenerate which may venture to serve the Holy One. He would not accept lodging or entertainment, acknowledgment, or blandishment, from the kingdom of darkness. He would not be made a king; He would not be called, Good Master; He would not accept where He might lay His head. His life lay not in man's breath, or man's smile; it was hid in Him from whom He came and to whom He returned.

"The Light shineth in darkness, and the darkness comprehended it not." He seemed like other men to the multitude. Though conceived of the Holy Ghost, He was born of a poor woman, who, when guests were numerous, was thrust aside, and gave birth to Him in a place for cattle. O wondrous mystery, early manifested, that even in birth He refused the world's welcome! He grew up as the carpenter's son, without education, so that when He began to teach, His neighbours wondered how one who had not learned letters, and was bred to a humble craft, should become a prophet. He was known as the kinsman and intimate of humble persons; so that the world pointed to them when He declared Himself, as if their insufficiency was the refutation of His claims. He was brought up in a town of low repute, so that even the better sort doubted whether good could come out of it. No; He would not be indebted to this world for comfort, aid, or credit; for "the world was made by Him, and the world knew Him not." He came to it as a benefactor, not as a guest; not to borrow from it, but to impart to it.

And when He grew up, and began to preach the kingdom of heaven, the Holy Jesus took no more from the world then than before. He chose the portion of those Saints who preceded and prefigured Him, Abraham, Moses, David, Elijah, and His forerunner John the Baptist. He lived at large, without the ties of home or peaceful dwelling; He lived as a pilgrim in the land of promise; He lived in the wilderness. Abraham had lived in tents in the country which his descendants were to enjoy. David had wandered for seven years up and down the same during Saul's persecutions. Moses had been a prisoner in the howling wilderness, all the way from Mount Sinai to the borders of Canaan. Elijah wandered back again from Carmel to Sinai. And the Baptist had remained in the desert from his youth. Such in like manner was our Lord's manner of life, during His ministry: He was now in Galilee, now in Judæa; He is found in the mountain, in the wilderness, and in the city; but He vouchsafed to take no home, not even His Almighty Father's Temple at Jerusalem.

Now all this is quite independent of the special objects of mercy which brought Him upon earth. Though He had still submitted Himself by an incomprehensible condescension to the death on the cross at length, yet why did He from the first so spurn this world, when He was not atoning for its sins? He might at least have had the blessedness of brethren who believed in Him; He might have been happy and revered at home; He might have had honour in His own country; He might have submitted but at last to what He chose from the first; He might have delayed

His voluntary sufferings till that hour when His Father's and His own will made Him the sacrifice for sin.

But He did otherwise; and thus He becomes a lesson to us who are His disciples. He, who was so separate from the world, so present with the Father even in the days of His flesh, calls upon us, His brethren, as we are in Him and He in the Father, to show that we really are what we have been made, by renouncing the world while in the world, and living as in the presence of God.

Let them consider this, who think the perfection of our nature still consists, as before the Spirit was given, in the exercise of all its separate functions, animal and mental, not in the subjection and sacrifice of what is inferior in us to what is more excellent. Christ, who is the beginning and pattern of the new creature, lived out of the body while He was in it. His death indeed was required as an expiation; but why was His life so mortified, if such austerity be not man's glory?

Let us at this season approach Him with awe and love, in whom resides all perfection, and from whom we are allowed to gain it. Let us come to the Sanctifier to be sanctified. Let us come to Him to learn our duty, and to receive grace to do it. At other seasons of the year we are reminded of watching, toiling, struggling, and suffering; but at this season we are reminded simply of God's gifts towards us sinners. "Not by works of righteousness which we have done, but according to His mercy He saved us." We are reminded that we can do nothing, and that God does everything. This is especially the season of grace. We come to see and to experience God's mercies. We come before Him as the helpless beings, during His ministry, who were brought on beds and couches for a cure. We come to be made whole. We come as little children to be fed and taught, "as new-born babes, desiring the sincere milk of the word, that we may grow thereby."[69] This is a time for innocence, and purity, and gentleness, and mildness, and contentment, and peace. It is a time in which the whole Church seems decked in white, in her baptismal robe, in the bright and glistering raiment which she wears upon the Holy Mount. Christ comes at other times with garments dyed in blood; but now He comes to us in all serenity and peace, and He bids us rejoice in Him, and to love one another. This is not a time for gloom, or jealousy, or care, or indulgence, or excess, or licence:— not for "rioting and drunkenness," not for "chambering and wantonness," not for "strife and envying,"[70] as says the Apostle; but for putting on the Lord Jesus Christ, "who knew no sin, neither was guile found in His mouth."

May each Christmas, as it comes, find us more and more like Him, who as at this time became a little child for our sake, more simple-minded, more humble, more holy, more affectionate, more resigned, more happy, more full of God.

---

[69] 1 Pet. 2:2
[70] Rom. 13:13

Christian Sympathy

"For verily He took not on Him the nature of Angels, but He took on Him the seed of Abraham." Heb. 2:16.

We are all of one nature, because we are sons of Adam; we are all of one nature, because we are brethren of Christ. Our old nature is common to us all, and so is our new nature. And because our old nature is one and the same, therefore is it that our new nature is one and the same. Christ could not have taken the nature of every one of us, unless every one of us had the same nature already. He could not have become our brother, unless we were all brethren already; He could not have made us His brethren, unless by becoming our Brother; so that our brotherhood in the first man is the means towards our brotherhood in the second.

I do not mean to limit the benefits of Christ's atoning death, or to dare to say that it may not effect ends infinite in number and extent beyond those expressly recorded. But still so far is plain, that it is by taking our nature that He has done for us what He has done for none else; that, by taking the nature of Angels, He would not have done for us what He has done; that it is not only the humiliation of the Son of God, but His humiliation in our nature, which is our life. He might have humbled Himself in other natures besides human nature; but it was decreed that "the Word" should be "made flesh." "Forasmuch as the children are partakers of flesh and blood, He also Himself likewise took part of the same." And, as the text says, "He took not hold of Angels, but He took hold of the seed of Abraham."[71]

And since His taking on Him our nature is a necessary condition of His imparting to us those great benefits which have accrued to us from His death, therefore, as I have said, it was necessary that we should, one and all, have the same original nature, in order to be redeemed by Him; for, in order to be redeemed, we must all have that nature which He the Redeemer took. Had our natures been different, He would have redeemed one and not another. Such a common nature we have, as being one and all children of one man, Adam; and thus the history of our fall is connected with the history of our recovery.

Christ then took our nature, when He would redeem it; He redeemed it by making it suffer in His own Person; He purified it, by making it pure in His own Person. He first sanctified it in Himself, made it righteous, made it acceptable to God, submitted it to an expiatory passion, and then He imparted it to us. He took it, consecrated it, broke it, and said, "Take, and divide it among yourselves."

And moreover, He raised the condition of human nature, by submitting it to trial and temptation; that what it failed to do in Adam, it might be able to do in Him. Or, in other words, which it becomes us rather to use, He condescended, by an ineffable mercy, to be tried and tempted in it; so that, whereas He was God from everlasting, as the Only-begotten of the Father,

---

[71] Heb. 2:14, 16

He took on Him the thoughts, affections, and infirmities of man, thereby, through the fulness of His Divine Nature, to raise those thoughts and affections, and destroy those infirmities, that so, by God's becoming man, men, through brotherhood with Him, might in the end become as gods.

There is not a feeling, not a passion, not a wish, not an infirmity, which we have, which did not belong to that manhood which He assumed, except such as is of the nature of sin. There was not a trial or temptation which befalls us, but was, in kind at least, presented before Him, except that He had nothing within Him, sympathizing with that which came to Him from without. He said upon His last and greatest trial, "The Prince of this world cometh and hath nothing in Me;" yet at the same time we are mercifully assured that "we have not a High Priest which cannot be touched with the feeling of our infirmities, but" one, who "was in all points tempted like as we are, yet without sin." And again, "In that He Himself hath suffered being tempted, He is able to succour them that are tempted."[72]

But what I would today draw attention to, is the thought with which I began, viz. the comfort vouchsafed to us in being able to contemplate Him whom the Apostle calls "the man Christ Jesus," the Son of God in our flesh. I mean, the thought of Him, "the beginning of the creation of God," "the firstborn of every creature," binds us together by a sympathy with one another, as much greater than that of mere nature,

---

[72] Heb. 4:15; Heb. 2:18

as Christ is greater than Adam. We were brethren, as being of one nature with him, who was "of the earth, earthy;" we are now brethren, as being of one nature with "the Lord from heaven." All those common feelings, which we have by birth, are far more intimately common to us, now that we have obtained the second birth. Our hopes and fears, likes and dislikes, pleasures and pains, have been moulded upon one model, have been wrought into one image, blended and combined unto "the measure of the stature of the fulness of Christ." What they become, who have partaken of "the Living Bread, which came down from heaven," the first converts showed, of whom it is said that they "had all things common;" that "the multitude of them that believed were of one heart and of one soul;" as having "one body, and one Spirit, one hope, one Lord, one Faith, one Baptism, one God and Father of all."[73] Yes, and one thing needful; one narrow way; one business on earth; one and the same enemy; the same dangers; the same temptations; the same afflictions; the same course of life; the same death; the same resurrection; the same judgment. All these things being the same, and the new nature being the same, and from the Same, no wonder that Christians can sympathise with each other, even as by the power of Christ sympathising in and with each of them.

Nay, and further, they sympathise together in those respects too, in which Christ has not, could not have, gone before them; I mean in their common sins. This is the difference between Christ's temptation and ours:

---

[73] Acts 2:44; Acts 4:32. Eph. 4:4-6

His temptations were without sin, but ours with sin. Temptation with us almost certainly involves sin. We sin, almost spontaneously, in spite of His grace. I do not mean, God forbid, that His grace is not sufficient to subdue all sin in us; or that, as we come more and more under its influence, we are not less and less exposed to the involuntary impression of temptation, and much less exposed to voluntary sin; but that so it is, our evil nature remains in us in spite of that new nature which the touch of Christ communicates to us; we have still earthly principles in our souls, though we have heavenly ones, and these so sympathise with temptation, that, as a mirror reflects promptly and of necessity what is presented to it, so the body of death which infects us, when the temptations of this world assail it,—when honour, pomp, glory, the world's praise, power, ease, indulgence, sensual pleasure, revenge are offered to it,—involuntarily responds to them, and sins —sins because it *is* sin; sins before the better mind can control it, because it exists, because its life is sin; sins *till* it is utterly subdued and expelled from the soul by the gradual growth of holiness and the power of the Spirit. Of all this, Christ had nothing. He was "born of a pure Virgin," the immaculate Lamb of God; and though He was tempted, yet it was by what was good in the world's offers, though unseasonable and unsuitable, and not by what was evil in them. He overcame what it had been unbecoming to yield to, while he felt the temptation. He overcame also what was sinful, but He felt no temptation to it.

And yet it stands to reason, that though His temptations differed from ours in this main respect, yet

His presence in us makes us sympathise one with another, even in our sins and faults, in a way which is impossible without it; because, whereas the grace in us is common to us all, the sins against that grace are common to us all also. We have the same gifts to sin against, and therefore the same powers, the same responsibilities, the same fears, the same struggles, the same guilt, the same repentance, and such as none can have but we. The Christian is one and the same, wherever found; as in Christ, who is perfect, so in himself, who is training towards perfection; as in that righteousness which is imputed to him in fulness, so in that righteousness which is imparted to him only in its measure, and not yet in fulness.

This is a consideration full of comfort, but of which commonly we do not avail ourselves as we might. It is one comfortable thought, and the highest of all, that Christ, who is on the right hand of God exalted, has felt all that we feel, sin excepted; but it is very comfortable also, that the new and spiritual man, which He creates in us, or creates us into,—that is, the Christian, as he is naturally found everywhere,—has everywhere the same temptations, and the same feelings under them, whether innocent or sinful; so that, as we are all bound together in our Head, so are we bound together, as members of one body, in that body, and believe, obey, sin, and repent, all in common.

I do not wish to state this too strongly. Doubtless there are very many differences between Christian and Christian. Though their nature is the same, and their general duties, hindrances, helps, privileges, and rewards the same, yet certainly there are great differences of character, and peculiarities belonging either to individuals or to classes. High and low, rich and poor, Jew and Gentile, man and woman, bond and free, learned and unlearned, though equal in the Gospel, do in many respects differ, so that descriptions of what passes in the mind of one will often appear strange and new to the other. Their temptations differ, and their diseases of mind. And the difference becomes far greater, by the difficulty persons have of expressing exactly what they mean, so that they convey wrong ideas to one another, and offend and repel those who really do feel what they feel, though they would express themselves otherwise.

Again, of course there is this great difference between Christians, that some are penitents, and some have never fallen away since they were brought near to God; some have fallen for a time, and grievously; others for long years, yet perhaps only in lesser matters. These circumstances will make real differences between Christian and Christian, so as sometimes even to remove the possibility of sympathy almost altogether. Sin certainly does contrive this victory in some cases, to hinder us being even fellows in misery; it separates us while it seduces, and, being the broad way, has different lesser tracks marked out upon it.

But still, after all such exceptions, I consider that Christians, certainly those who are in the same outward circumstances, are very much more like each other in their temptations, inward diseases, and methods of cure, than they at all imagine. Persons think themselves isolated in the world; they think no one ever felt as they feel. They do not dare to expose their feelings, lest they should find that no one understands them. And thus they suffer to wither and decay what was destined in God's purpose to adorn the Church's paradise with beauty and sweetness. Their "mouth is not opened," as the Apostle speaks, nor their "heart enlarged;" they are "straitened" in themselves, and deny themselves the means they possess of at once imparting instruction and gaining comfort.

Nay, instead of speaking out their own thoughts, they suffer the world's opinion to hang upon them as a load, or the influence of some system of religion which is in vogue. It very frequently happens that ten thousand people all say what not any one of them feels, but each says it because every one else says it, and each fears not to say it lest he should incur the censure of all the rest. Such are very commonly what are called the opinions of the age. They are bad principles or doctrines, or false notions or views, which live in the mouths of men, and have their strength in their public recognition. Of course by proud men, or blind, or carnal, or worldly, these opinions which I speak of are really felt and entered into; for they are the natural growth of their own evil hearts. But very frequently the same are set forth, and heralded, and circulated, and become current opinions, among vast multitudes of men who do not feel them. These multitudes, however, are obliged to receive them by what is called the force of public opinion; the careless of course, carelessly, but the better sort superstitiously. Thus ways of speech come in, and modes of thought quite alien to the minds of those who give in to them, who feel them to be unreal, unnatural, and uncongenial to themselves, but consider themselves obliged, often from the most religious principles, not to confess their feelings about them. They dare not say, they dare not even realize to themselves their own judgments. Thus it is that the world cuts off the intercourse between soul and soul, and substitutes idols of its own for the one true Image of Christ, in and through which only souls can sympathise. Their best thoughts are stifled, and when by chance they hear them put forth elsewhere, as may sometimes be the case, they feel as it were conscious and guilty, as if some one were revealing something against them, and they shrink from the sound as from a temptation, as something pleasing indeed but forbidden. Such is the power of false creeds to fetter the mind and bring it into captivity; false views of things, of facts, of doctrines, are imposed on it tyrannically, and men live and die in bondage, who were destined to rise to the stature of the fulness of Christ. Such, for example, I consider to be, among many instances, the interpretation which is popularly received among us at present, of the doctrinal portion of St. Paul's Epistles, an interpretation which has troubled large portions of the Church for a long three hundred years.

But, I repeat, we are much more like each other, even in our sins, than we fancy. I do not of course mean to say, that we are one and all at the same point in our Christian course, or have one and all had the same religious history in times past; but that, even taking a man who has never fallen from grace, and one who has fallen most grievously and repented, even they will be found to be very much more like each other in their view of themselves, in their temptations, and feelings upon those temptations, than they might fancy beforehand. This we see most strikingly instanced when holy men set about to describe their real state. Even bad men at once cry out, "This is just our case," and argue from it that there is no difference between bad and good. They impute all their own sins to the holiest of men, as making their own lives a sort of comment upon the text which his words furnish, and appealing to the appositeness of their own interpretation in proof of its correctness. And I suppose it cannot be denied, concerning all of us, that we are generally surprised to hear the strong language which good men use of themselves, as if such confessions showed them to be more like ourselves, and much less holy than we had fancied them to be. And on the other hand, I suppose, any man of tolerably correct life, whatever his positive advancement in grace, will seldom read accounts of notoriously bad men, in which their ways and feelings are described, without being shocked to find that these more or less cast a meaning upon his own heart, and bring out into light and colour lines and shapes of thought within him, which, till then, were almost invisible. Now this does not show that bad and good men are on a level, but it shows this, that they are of the same nature. It shows that the one has within him in tendency, what the other has brought out into actual existence; so that the good has nothing to boast of over the bad, and while what is good in him is from God's grace, there is an abundance left, which marks him as being beyond all doubt of one blood with those sons of Adam who are still far from Christ their Redeemer. And if this is true of bad and good, much more is it true in the case of which I am speaking, that is of good men one with another; of penitents and the upright. They understand each other far more than might at first have been supposed. And whereas their sense of the heinousness of sin rises with their own purity, those who are holiest will speak of themselves in the same terms as impure persons use about themselves; so that Christians, though they really differ much, yet as regards the power of sympathising with each other will be found to be on a level. The one is not too high or the other too low. They have common ground; and as they have one faith and hope, and one Spirit, so also they have one and the same circle of temptations, and one and the same confession.

It were well if we understood all this. Perhaps the reason why the standard of holiness among us is so low, why our attainments are so poor, our view of the truth so dim, our belief so unreal, our general notions so artificial and external is this, that we dare not trust each other with the secret of our hearts. We have each the same secret, and we keep it to ourselves, and we fear that, as a cause of estrangement, which really would be a bond of union. We do not probe the wounds of our nature thoroughly; we do not lay the foundation of our religious profession in the ground of our inner man; we make clean the outside of things; we are amiable and friendly to each other in words and deeds, but our love is not enlarged, our bowels of affection are straitened, and we fear to let the intercourse begin at the root; and, in consequence, our religion, viewed as a social system, is hollow. The presence of Christ is not in it.

To conclude. If it be awful to tell to another in our own way what we are, what will be the awfulness of that Day when the secrets of all hearts shall be disclosed! Let us ever bear this in mind when we fear that others should know what we are really:—whether we are right or wrong in hiding our sins now, it is a vain notion if we suppose they will always be hidden. The Day shall declare it; the Lord will come in Judgment; He "will bring to light the hidden things of darkness, and will make manifest the counsels of the hearts."[74] With this thought before us, surely it is a little thing whether or not man knows us here. *Then* will be knowledge without sympathy: then will be shame with everlasting contempt. Now, though there be shame, there is comfort and a soothing relief; though there be awe, it is greater on the side of him who hears than of him who makes avowal.

---

[74] 1 Cor. 4:5

Religious Joy

"And the angels said unto them, Fear not: for, behold, I bring you good tidings of great joy, which shall be to all people. For unto you is born this day in the city of David a Saviour, which is Christ the Lord." Luke 2:10-11.

There are two principal lessons which we are taught on the great Festival which we this day celebrate, lowliness and joy. This surely is a day, of all others, in which is set before us the heavenly excellence and the acceptableness in God's sight of that state which most men have, or may have, allotted to them, humble or private life, and cheerfulness in it. If we consult the writings of historians, philosophers, and poets of this world, we shall be led to think great men happy; we shall be led to fix our minds and hearts upon high or conspicuous stations, strange adventures, powerful talents to cope with them, memorable struggles, and great destinies. We shall consider that the highest course of life is the mere pursuit, not the enjoyment of good.

But when we think of this day's Festival, and what we commemorate upon it, a new and very different scene opens upon us. First, we are reminded that though this life must ever be a life of toil and effort, yet that, properly speaking, we have not to seek our highest good. It is found, it is brought near us, in the descent of the Son of God from His Father's bosom to this world. It is stored up among us on earth. No longer need men of ardent minds weary themselves in the pursuit of what they fancy may be chief goods; no longer have they to wander about and encounter peril in quest of that unknown blessedness to which their hearts naturally aspire, as they did in heathen times. The text speaks to them and to all, "Unto you," it says, "is born this day in the city of David a Saviour, which is Christ the Lord."

Nor, again, need we go in quest of any of those things which this vain world calls great and noble. Christ altogether dishonoured what the world esteems, when He took on Himself a rank and station which the world despises. No lot could be more humble and more ordinary than that which the Son of God chose for Himself.

So that we have on the Feast of the Nativity these two lessons—instead of anxiety within and despondence without, instead of a weary search after great things,—to be cheerful and joyful; and, again, to be so in the midst of those obscure and ordinary circumstances of life which the world passes over and thinks scorn of.

Let us consider this more at length, as contained in the gracious narrative of which the text is part.

1. First, what do we read just before the text? that there were certain shepherds keeping watch over their flock by night, and Angels appeared to them. Why should the heavenly hosts appear to these shepherds? What was it in them which attracted the attention of the Angels and the Lord of Angels? Were these shepherds learned, distinguished, or powerful? Were they especially known for piety and gifts? Nothing is said to make us think so. Faith, we may safely say, they had, or some of them, for to him that hath more shall

be given; but there is nothing to show that they were holier and more enlightened than other good men of the time, who waited for the consolation of Israel. Nay, there is no reason to suppose that they were better than the common run of men in their circumstances, simple, and fearing God, but without any great advances in piety, or any very formed habits of religion. Why then were they chosen? for their poverty's sake and obscurity. Almighty God looks with a sort of especial love, or (as we may term it) affection, upon the lowly. Perhaps it is that man, a fallen, dependent, and destitute creature, is more in his proper place when he is in lowly circumstances, and that power and riches, though unavoidable in the case of some, are unnatural appendages to man, as such. Just as there are trades and callings which are unbecoming, though requisite; and while we profit by them, and honour those the more who engage in them, yet we feel we are glad that they are not ours; as we feel grateful and respectful towards a soldier's profession, yet do not affect it; so in God's sight greatness is less acceptable than obscurity. It becomes us less.

The shepherds, then, were chosen on account of their lowliness, to be the first to hear of the Lord's nativity, a secret which none of the princes of this world knew.

And what a contrast is presented to us when we take into account who were our Lord's messengers to them! The Angels who excel in strength, these did His bidding towards the shepherds. Here the highest and the lowest of God's rational creatures are brought together. A set of poor men, engaged in a life of hardship, exposed at that very time to the cold and darkness of the night, watching their flocks, with the view of scaring away beasts of prey or robbers; they—when they are thinking of nothing but earthly things, counting over the tale of their sheep, keeping their dogs by their side, and listening to the noises over the plain, considering the weather and watching for the day—suddenly are met by far other visitants than they conceived. We know the contracted range of thought, the minute and ordinary objects, or rather the one or two objects, to and fro again and again without variety, which engage the minds of men exposed to such a life of heat, cold, and wet, hunger and nakedness, hardship and servitude. They cease to care much for any thing, but go on in a sort of mechanical way, without heart, and still more without reflection.

To men so circumstanced the Angel appeared, to open their minds, and to teach them not to be downcast and in bondage because they were low in the world. He appeared as if to show them that God had chosen the poor in this world to be heirs of His kingdom, and so to do honour to their lot. "Fear not," he said, "for behold I bring you good tidings of great joy, which shall be to all people. For unto you is born this day in the city of David a Saviour, which is Christ the Lord."

2. And now comes a second lesson, which I have said may be gained from the Festival. The Angel honoured a humble lot by his very appearing to the shepherds; next he taught it to be joyful by his message. He disclosed good tidings so much above this world as

to equalize high and low, rich and poor, one with another. He said, "Fear not." This is a mode of address frequent in Scripture, as you may have observed, as if man needed some such assurance to support him, especially in God's presence. The Angel said, "Fear not," when he saw the alarm which his presence caused among the shepherds. Even a lesser wonder would have reasonably startled them. Therefore the Angel said, "Fear not." We are naturally afraid of any messenger from the other world, for we have an uneasy conscience when left to ourselves, and think that his coming forebodes evil. Besides, we so little realize the unseen world, that were Angel or spirit to present himself before us we should be startled by reason of our unbelief, a truth being brought home to our minds which we never apprehended before. So for one or other reason the shepherds were sore afraid when the glory of the Lord shone around about them. And the Angel said, "Fear not." A little religion makes us afraid; when a little light is poured in upon the conscience, there is a darkness visible; nothing but sights of woe and terror; the glory of God alarms while it shines around. His holiness, the range and difficulties of His commandments, the greatness of His power, the faithfulness of His word, frighten the sinner, and men seeing him afraid, think religion has made him so, whereas he is not yet religious at all. They call him religious, when he is merely conscience-stricken. But religion itself, far from inculcating alarm and terror, says, in the words of the Angel, "Fear not;" for such is His mercy, while Almighty God has poured about us His glory, yet it is a consolatory glory, for it is the light of His glory in the Face of Jesus Christ.[75] Thus the heavenly herald tempered the too dazzling brightness of the Gospel on that first Christmas. The glory of God at first alarmed the shepherds, so he added the tidings of good, to work in them a more wholesome and happy temper. Then they rejoiced.

"Fear not," said the Angel, "for behold I bring you good tidings of great joy, which shall be to all people. For unto you is born this day in the city of David a Saviour, which is Christ the Lord." And then, when he had finished his announcement, "suddenly there was with the Angel a multitude of the heavenly host, praising God and saying, Glory to God in the highest, and on earth peace, good will towards men." Such were the words which the blessed Spirits who minister to Christ and His Saints, spoke on that gracious night to the shepherds, to rouse them out of their cold and famished mood into great joy; to teach them that they were objects of God's love as much as the greatest of men on earth; nay more so, for to them first He had imparted the news of what that night was happening. His Son was then born into the world. Such events are told to friends and intimates, to those whom we love, to those who will sympathize with us, not to strangers. How could Almighty God be more gracious, and show His favour more impressively to the lowly and the friendless, than by hastening (if I may use the term) to confide the great, the joyful secret to the shepherds keeping watch over their sheep by night?

---

[75] 2 Cor. 4:6

The Angel then gave the first lesson of mingled humility and joyfulness; but an infinitely greater one was behind in the event itself, to which he directed the shepherds, in that birth itself of the Holy Child Jesus. This he intimated in these words: "Ye shall find the babe wrapped in swaddling clothes, lying in a manger." Doubtless, when they heard the Lord's Christ was born into the world, they would look for Him in kings' palaces. They would not be able to fancy that He had become one of themselves, or that they might approach Him; therefore the Angel thus warned them where to find Him, not only as a sign, but as a lesson also.

"The shepherds said one to another, Let us now go even unto Bethlehem, and see this thing which is come to pass, which the Lord hath made known to us." Let us too go with them, to contemplate that second and greater miracle to which the Angel directed them, the Nativity of Christ. St. Luke says of the Blessed Virgin, "She brought forth her first-born Son, and wrapped Him in swaddling clothes, and laid Him in a manger." What a wonderful sign is this to all the world, and therefore the Angel repeated it to the shepherds: "Ye shall find the babe wrapped in swaddling clothes, lying in a manger." The God of heaven and earth, the Divine Word, who had been in glory with the Eternal Father from the beginning, He was at this time born into this world of sin as a little infant. He, as at this time, lay in His mother's arms, to all appearance helpless and powerless, and was wrapped by Mary in an infant's bands, and laid to sleep in a manger. The Son of God Most High, who created the worlds, became flesh, though remaining what He was before. He became flesh as truly as if He had ceased to be what He was, and had actually been changed into flesh. He submitted to be the offspring of Mary, to be taken up in the hands of a mortal, to have a mother's eye fixed upon Him, and to be cherished at a mother's bosom. A daughter of man became the Mother of God—to her, indeed, an unspeakable gift of grace; but in Him what condescension! What an emptying of His glory to become man! and not only a helpless infant, though that were humiliation enough, but to inherit all the infirmities and imperfections of our nature which were possible to a sinless soul. What were His thoughts, if we may venture to use such language or admit such a reflection concerning the Infinite, when human feelings, human sorrows, human wants, first became His? What a mystery is there from first to last in the Son of God becoming man! Yet in proportion to the mystery is the grace and mercy of it; and as is the grace, so is the greatness of the fruit of it.

Let us steadily contemplate the mystery, and say whether any consequence is too great to follow from so marvellous a dispensation; any mystery so great, any grace so overpowering, as that which is already manifested in the incarnation and death of the Eternal Son. Were we told that the effect of it would be to make us as Seraphim, that we were to ascend as high as He descended low—would that startle us after the Angel's news to the shepherds? And this indeed is the effect of it, so far as such words may be spoken without impiety. Men we remain, but not mere men, but gifted with a measure of all those perfections which Christ has in fulness, partaking each in his own degree of His Divine Nature so fully, that the only reason (so to speak) why His saints are not really like Him, is that it is impossible—that He is the Creator, and they His creatures; yet still so, that they are all but Divine, all that they can be made without violating the incommunicable majesty of the Most High. Surely in proportion to His glory is His power of glorifying; so that to say that through Him we shall be made *all but* gods—though it is to say, that we are infinitely below the adorable Creator—still is to say, and truly, that we shall be higher than every other being in the world; higher than Angels or Archangels, Cherubim or Seraphim—that is, not here, or in ourselves, but in heaven and in Christ:— Christ, already the first-fruits of our race, God and man, having ascended high above all creatures, and we through His grace tending to the same high blessedness, having the earnest of His glory given here, and (if we be found faithful) the fulness of it hereafter.

If all these things be so, surely the lesson of joy which the Incarnation gives us is as impressive as the lesson of humility. St. Paul gives us the one lesson in his epistle to the Philippians: "Let this mind be in you, which was also in Christ Jesus: who, being in the form of God, thought it not robbery to be equal with God: but made Himself of no reputation, and took upon Him the form of a servant, and was made in the likeness of men:" and St. Peter gives us the lesson of joyfulness: "whom having not seen, ye love; in whom, though now ye see Him not, yet believing, ye rejoice with joy unspeakable, and full of glory: receiving the end of your faith, even the salvation of your souls."[76]

Take these thoughts with you, my brethren, to your homes on this festive day; let them be with you in your family and social meetings. It is a day of joy: it is good to be joyful—it is wrong to be otherwise. For one day we may put off the burden of our polluted consciences, and rejoice in the perfections of our Saviour Christ, without thinking of ourselves, without thinking of our own miserable uncleanness; but contemplating His glory, His righteousness, His purity, His majesty, His overflowing love. We may rejoice in the Lord, and in all His creatures see Him. We may enjoy His temporal bounty, and partake the pleasant things of earth with Him in our thoughts; we may rejoice in our friends for His sake, loving them most especially because He has loved them.

"God has not appointed us unto wrath, but to obtain salvation through our Lord Jesus Christ, who died for us, that whether we wake or sleep, we should live together with Him." Let us seek the grace of a cheerful heart, an even temper, sweetness, gentleness, and brightness of mind, as walking in His light, and by His grace. Let us pray Him to give us the spirit of ever-abundant, ever-springing love, which overpowers and sweeps away the vexations of life by its own richness and strength, and which above all things unites us to Him who is the fountain and the centre of all mercy, lovingkindness, and joy.

---

[76] Phil. 2:5-7; 1 Pet. 1:8-9

The Glory of the Christian Church

"Arise, shine; for thy light is come, and the glory of the Lord is risen upon thee." Isaiah 60:1.

Our Saviour said to the woman of Samaria, "The hour cometh, when ye shall neither in this mountain, nor yet at Jerusalem, worship the Father."[77] And upon today's Festival I may say to you in His words on another occasion, "This day is this scripture fulfilled in your ears." This day we commemorate the opening of the door of faith to the Gentiles, the extension of the Church of God through all lands, whereas, before Christ's coming, it had been confined to one nation only. This dissemination of the Truth throughout the world had been the subject of prophecy. "Enlarge the place of thy tent, and let them stretch forth the curtains of thine habitations: spare not, lengthen thy cords, and strengthen thy stakes; for thou shalt break forth on the right hand and on the left; and thy seed shall inherit the Gentiles, and make the desolate cities to be inhabited."[78] In these words the Church is addressed as Catholic, which is the distinguishing title of the Christian Church, as contrasted with the Jewish. The Christian Church is so constituted as to be able to spread itself out in its separate branches into all regions of the earth; so that in every nation there may be found a representative and an offshoot of the sacred and gifted Society, set up once for all by our Lord after His resurrection.

---

[77] John 4:21
[78] Isa. 54:2-3

This characteristic blessing of the Church of Christ, its Catholic nature, is a frequent subject of rejoicing with St. Paul, who was the chief instrument of its propagation. In one Epistle he speaks of Gentiles being "fellow heirs" with the Jews, "and of the same body, and partakers of His promise in Christ by the Gospel." In another he enlarges on "the mystery now made manifest to the saints," viz. "Christ among the Gentiles, the hope of glory."[79]

The day on which we commemorate this gracious appointment of God's Providence, is called the Epiphany, or bright manifestation of Christ to the Gentiles; being the day on which the wise men came from the East under guidance of a star, to worship Him, and thus became the first-fruits of the heathen world. The name is explained by the words of the text, which occur in one of the lessons selected for today's service, and in which the Church is addressed. "Arise, shine; for thy light is come, and the glory of the Lord is risen upon thee. For, behold, the darkness shall cover the earth, and gross darkness the people: but the Lord shall arise upon thee, and His glory shall be seen upon thee. And the Gentiles shall come to thy light, and kings to the brightness of thy rising... Thy people also shall be all righteous: they shall inherit the land for ever, the branch of My planting, the work of My hands, that I may be glorified."[80]

That this and other similar prophecies had their measure of fulfilment when Christ came, we all know;

---

[79] Eph. 3:6; Col. 1:26-27
[80] Isa. 60:1-3, 21

when His Church, built upon the Apostles and Prophets, wonderfully branched out from Jerusalem as a centre into the heathen world round about, and gathering into it men of all ranks, languages, and characters, moulded them upon one pattern, the pattern of their Saviour, in truth and righteousness. Thus the prophecies concerning the Church were fulfilled at that time in two respects, as regards its sanctity and its Catholicity.

It is often asked, have these prophecies had then and since their perfect accomplishment? Or are we to expect a more complete Christianizing of the world than has hitherto been vouchsafed it? And it is usual at the present day to acquiesce in the latter alternative, as if the inspired predictions certainly meant more than has yet been realized.

Now so much, I think, is plain on the face of them, that the Gospel is to be preached in all lands, before the end comes: "This gospel of the kingdom shall be preached in all the world for a witness unto all nations; and then shall the end come."[81] Whether it has been thus preached is a question of fact, which must be determined, not from the prophecy, but from history; and there we may leave it. But as to the other expectation, that a time of greater purity is in store for the Church, that is not easily to be granted. The very words of Christ just quoted, so far from speaking of the Gospel as tending to the conversion of the world at large, when preached in it, describe it only as a *witness* unto all the Gentiles, as if the many would not obey it.

81 Matt. 24:14

And this intimation runs parallel to St. Paul's account of the Jewish Church, as realizing faith and obedience only in a residue out of the whole people; and is further illustrated by St. John's language in the Apocalypse, who speaks of the "redeemed from among men" being but a remnant, "the first-fruits unto God and to the Lamb."[82]

However, I will readily allow that at first we shall feel a reluctance in submitting to this opinion, with such passages before us as that which occurs in the eleventh chapter of Isaiah's prophecy, where it is promised, "They shall not hurt nor destroy in all My holy mountain; for the earth shall be full of the knowledge of the Lord, as the waters cover the sea."[83] I say it is natural, with such texts in the memory, to look out for what is commonly called a Millennium. It may be instructive then upon this day to make some remarks in explanation of the state and prospects of the Christian Church in this respect.

Now the system of this world depends, in a way unknown to us, both on God's Providence and on human agency. Every event, every course of action, has two faces; it is divine and perfect, and it belongs to man and is marked with his sin. I observe next, that it is a peculiarity of Holy Scripture to represent the world on its providential side; ascribing all that happens in it to Him who rules and directs it, as it moves along, tracing events to His sole agency, or viewing them only so far forth as He acts in them. Thus He is said to harden

---

[82] Rom. 11:5; Rev. 14:4
[83] Isa. 11:9

Pharaoh's heart, and to hinder the Jews from believing in Christ; wherein is signified His absolute sovereignty over all human affairs and courses. As common is it for Scripture to consider Dispensations, not in their actual state, but as His agency would mould them, and so far as it really does succeed in moulding them. For instance: "God, who is rich in mercy, for His great love wherewith He loved us, even when we were dead in sins, hath quickened us together with Christ."[84] This is said as if the Ephesians had no traces left in their hearts of Adam's sin and spiritual death. As it is said afterwards, "Ye were sometimes darkness, but now are ye light in the Lord."[85]

In other words, Scripture more commonly speaks of the Divine *design* and *substantial work*, than of the *measure* of fulfilment which it receives at this time or that; as St. Paul expresses, when he says that the Ephesians were chosen, that they "*should* be holy and unblameable before Him in love." Or it speaks of the *profession* of the Christian; as when he says, "As many of you as have been baptized in Christ, have put on Christ;"—or of the *tendency* of the Divine gift in a long period of time, and of its *ultimate fruits*; as in the words, "Christ loved the Church, and gave Himself for it, that He might sanctify and cleanse it with the washing of water by the word, that He might present to Himself a glorious Church, not having spot, or wrinkle, or any such thing, but that it should be holy and without blemish,"[86] in

---

[84] Eph. 2:4-5
[85] Eph. 5:8
[86] Eph. 1:4; Gal. 3:27; Eph. 5:25-27

which baptism and final salvation are viewed as if indissolubly connected. This rule of Scripture interpretation admits of very extensive application, and I proceed to illustrate it.

The principle under consideration is this: that, whereas God is one, and His will one, and His purpose one, and His work one; whereas all He is and does is absolutely perfect and complete, independent of time and place, and sovereign over creation, whether inanimate or living, yet that in His actual dealings with this world that is, in all in which we see His Providence (in that man is imperfect, and has a will of his own, and lives in time, and is moved by circumstances), He seems to work by a process, by means and ends, by steps, by victories hardly gained, and failures repaired, and sacrifices ventured. Thus it is only when we view His dispensations at a distance, as the Angels do, that we see their harmony and their unity; whereas Scripture, anticipating the end from the beginning, places at their very head and first point of origination all that belongs to them respectively in their fulness.

We find some exemplification of this principle in the call of Abraham. In every age of the world it has held good that the just shall live by faith; yet it was determined in the deep counsels of God, that for a while this truth should be partially obscured, as far as His revelations went; that man should live by sight, miracles and worldly ordinances taking the place of silent providences and spiritual services. In the latter times of the Jewish Law the original doctrine was brought to light, and when the Divine Object of faith was born into the world, it was authoritatively set forth by His Apostles as the basis of all acceptable worship. But observe, it had been already anticipated in the instance of Abraham; the evangelical covenant, which was not to be preached till near two thousand years afterwards, was revealed and transacted in his person. "Abraham believed God, and it was counted unto him for righteousness." "Abraham rejoiced to see My day; and he saw it, and was glad."[87] Nay, in the commanded sacrifice of his beloved son, was shadowed out the true Lamb which God had provided for a burnt offering. Thus in the call of the Patriarch, in whose Seed all nations of the earth should be blessed, the great outlines of the Gospel were anticipated; in that he was called in uncircumcision, that he was justified by faith, that he trusted in God's power to raise the dead, that he looked forward to the day of Christ, and that he was vouchsafed a vision of the Atoning Sacrifice on Calvary.

We call these notices *prophecy*, popularly speaking, and doubtless such they are to us, and to be received and used thankfully; but more properly, perhaps, they are merely instances of the harmonious movement of God's word and deed, His sealing up events from the first, His introducing them once and for all, though they are but gradually unfolded to our limited faculties, and in this transitory scene. It would seem that at the time when Abraham was called, both the course of the Jewish dispensation and the coming of Christ were (so to say) realized; so as, in one sense, to be actually done

---

[87] Rom. 4:3; John 8:56

and over. Hence, in one passage, Christ is called "the Lamb slain from the foundation of the world;" in another, it is said, that "Levi paid tithes" to Melchizedek, "in Abraham."[88]

Similar remarks might be made on the call and reign of David, and the building of the second Temple.

In like manner the Christian Church had in the day of its nativity all that fulness of holiness and peace named upon it, and sealed up to it, which beseemed it, viewed as God's design,—viewed in its essence, as it is realized at all times and under whatever circumstances, —viewed as God's work without man's co-operation,— viewed as God's work in its tendency, and in its ultimate blessedness; so that the titles given it upon earth are a picture of what it will be absolutely in heaven. This might also be instanced in the case of the Jewish Church, as in Jeremiah's description: "I remember thee, the kindness of thy youth, the love of thine espousals, when thou wentest after Me in the wilderness, in a land that was not sown. Israel was holiness unto the Lord, and the first-fruits of His increase."[89] As to the Christian Church, one passage descriptive of its blessedness from its first founding has already been cited; to which I add the following by way of specimen: "The Gentiles shall see thy righteousness, and all kings thy glory; and thou shalt be called by a new name, which the mouth of the Lord shall name. Thou shalt also be a crown of glory in the hand of the Lord, and a royal diadem in the hand of thy God... As the

---

88 Rev. 13:8; Heb. 7:9
89 Jer. 2:2-3

bridegroom rejoiceth over the bride, so shall thy God rejoice over thee." "The mountains shall depart, and the hills be removed; but My kindness shall not depart from thee, neither shall the covenant of My peace be removed, saith the Lord that hath mercy on thee. All thy children shall be taught of the Lord, and great shall be the peace of thy children." "Behold, I have graven thee upon the palms of My hands; thy walls are continually before Me... Lift up thine eyes round about, and behold; all these gather themselves together, and come to thee. As I live, saith the Lord, thou shalt surely clothe thee with them all, as with an ornament, and bind them on thee as a bride doeth." "Violence shall no more be heard in thy land, wasting nor destruction within thy borders; but thou shalt call thy walls salvation, and thy gates praise."[90] In these passages, which in their context certainly refer to the time of Christ's coming, an universality and a purity are promised to the Church, which have their fulfilment only in the course of its history, from first to last, as fore-shortened and viewed as one whole.

Consider, again, the representations given us of Christ's Kingdom. First, it is called the "Kingdom of *Heaven*," though on earth. Again, in the Angels' hymn, it is proclaimed "on earth peace," in accordance with the prophetic description of the Messiah as "the Prince of Peace;" though He Himself, speaking of the earthly, not the Divine side of His dispensation, said, He came "not to send peace on earth, but a sword."[91] Further,

---

[90] Isa. 62:3, 5; Isa. 54:10, 13; Isa. 44:16, 18; 60:18
[91] Matt. 10:34

consider Gabriel's announcement to the Virgin concerning her Son and Lord: "He shall be great, and shall be called the Son of the Highest; and the Lord God shall give unto Him the throne of His father David; and He shall reign over the house of Jacob for ever, and of His kingdom there shall be no end." Or, as the same Saviour had been foretold by Ezekiel: "I will set up one Shepherd over them, and He shall feed them... I will make with them a covenant of peace, and will cause the evil beasts to cease out of the land: and they shall dwell safely in the wilderness, and sleep in the woods. And I will make them and the places round about My hill a blessing; and I will cause the shower to come down in his season; there shall be showers of blessing."[92] It is observable that in the two passages last cited, the Christian Church is considered as merely the continuation of the Jewish, as if the Gospel existed in its germ even under the Law.

Now it is undeniable, and so blessed a truth that one would not wish at all to question it, that when Christ first came, His followers were in a state of spiritual purity, far above anything which we witness in the Church at this day. That glory with which her face shone, as Moses' of old time, from communion with her Saviour on the holy Mount, is the earnest of what will one day be perfected; it is a token held out to us in our dark age, that His promise stands sure, and admits of accomplishment. They continued in "gladness and singleness of heart, praising God, and having favour with all the people." Here was a pledge of eternal

---

92 Luke 1:32-33; Ezek. 34:23, 25, 26

blessedness, the same in kind as a child's innocence is a forerunner of a holy immortality; and as the baptismal robe of the fine linen, clean and white, which is the righteousness of saints;—a pledge like the typical promises made to David, Solomon, Cyrus, or Joshua the high-priest. Yet at the same time the corruptions in the early Church, Galatian misbelief, and Corinthian excess, show too clearly that her early glories were not more than a pledge, except in the case of individuals,— a pledge of God's purpose, a witness of man's depravity.

The same interpretation will apply to the Scripture account of the Elect People of God, which is but the Church of Christ under another name. On them, upon their election, are bestowed, as on a body, the gifts of justification, holiness, and final salvation. The perfections of Christ are shed around them; His image is reflected from them; so that they receive His name as being in Him, and beloved of God in the Beloved. Thus in their election are sealed up, to be unrolled and enjoyed in due season, the successive privileges of the heirs of light. In God's *purpose*—according to His *grace*—in the *tendency* and ultimate effects of his dispensation—to be called and chosen is to be saved. "Whom He did foreknow, He also did predestinate; whom He did predestinate, them He also called; whom He called, them He also justified; whom He justified, them He also glorified."[93] Observe, the whole scheme is spoken of as of a thing past; for in His deep counsel He contemplated from everlasting the one entire work, and,

---

[93] Rom. 8:29-30

having decreed it, it is but a matter of time, of sooner or later, when it will be realized. As the Lamb was slain from the foundation of the world, so also were His redeemed gathered in from the first according to His foreknowledge; and it is not more inconsistent with the solemn announcement of the text just cited, that some once elected should fall away (as we know they do), than that an event should be spoken of in it as past and perfect, which is incomplete and future. All accidents are excluded, when He speaks; the present and the to come, delays and failures, vanish before the thought of His perfect work. And hence it happens that the word "elect" in Scripture has two senses, standing both for those who are called *in order* to salvation, and for those who at the last day shall be the *actually resulting fruit* of that holy call. For God's Providence moves by great and comprehensive laws; and His word is the mirror of His designs, not of man's partial success in thwarting His gracious will.

The Church then, considered as one army militant, proceeding forward from the house of bondage to Canaan, gains the victory, and accomplishes what is predicted of her, though many soldiers fall in the battle. While, however, they remain within her lines, they are included in her blessedness so far as to be partakers of the gifts flowing from election. And hence it is that so much stress is to be laid upon the duty of united worship; for thus the multitude of believers coming together, claim as one man the grace which is poured out upon the one undivided body of Christ mystical. "Where two or three are gathered together in His name, He is in the midst of them;" nay rather, blessed be His name! He is so one with them, that they are not their own, lose for the time their earth-stains, are radiant in His infinite holiness, and have the promise of His eternal favour. Viewed as one, the Church is still His image as at the first, pure and spotless, His spouse all-glorious within, the Mother of Saints; according to the Scripture, "My dove, My undefiled is but one; she is the only one of her mother, she is the elect one of her that bare her... Thou art all fair, My love; there is no spot in thee."[94]

And what is true of the Church as a whole, is represented in Scripture as belonging also in some sense to each individual in it. I mean, that as the Christian body was set up in the image of Christ, which is gradually and in due season to be realized within it, so in like manner each of us, when made a Christian, is entrusted with gifts, which centre in eternal salvation. St. Peter says, we are "saved" through baptism; St. Paul, that we are "saved" according to God's mercy by "the washing of regeneration;" our Lord joins together water and the Spirit; St. Paul connects baptism with putting on Christ; and in another place with being "sanctified and justified in the name of the Lord Jesus, and by the Spirit of our God."[95] To the same purport are our Lord's words: "He that heareth My word, and believeth on Him that sent Me, *hath* everlasting life, and shall not come into condemnation, but *is passed* from death unto life."[96]

---

[94] Cant. 6:9; Cant. 4:7
[95] 1 Pet. 3:21; Tit. 3:5; John 3:5; Gal. 3:27; 1 Cor. 6:11
[96] John 5:24

These remarks have been made with a view of showing the true sense in which we must receive, on the one hand, the prophetic descriptions of the Christian Church; on the other, the grant of its privileges, and of those of its separate members. Nothing is more counter to the spirit of the Gospel than to hunger after signs and wonders; and the rule of Scripture interpretation now given, is especially adapted to wean us from such wanderings of heart. It is our duty, rather it is our blessedness, to walk by faith; therefore we will take the promises (with God's help) in faith; we will believe they are fulfilled, and enjoy the fruit of them before we see it. We will fully acknowledge, as being firmly persuaded, that His word cannot return unto Him void; that it has its mission, and must prosper so far as substantially to accomplish it. We will adore the Blessed Spirit as coming and going as He listeth, and doing wonders daily which the world knows not of. We will consider Baptism and the other Christian Ordinances effectual signs of grace, not forms and shadows, though men abuse and profane them; and particularly, as regards our immediate subject, we will unlearn, as sober and serious men, the expectation of any public displays of God's glory in the edification of His Church, seeing she is all-glorious *within*, in that inward shrine, made up of faithful hearts, and inhabited by the Spirit of grace. We will put off, so be it, all secular, all political views of the victories of His kingdom. While labouring to unite its fragments, which the malice of Satan has scattered to and fro, to recover what is cast away, to purify what is corrupted, to strengthen what is weak, to make it in all its parts what Christ would have it, a Church Militant, still (please God) we will not reckon on any visible fruit of our labour. We will be content to believe our cause triumphant, when we see it apparently defeated. We will silently bear the insults of the enemies of Christ, and resign ourselves meekly to the shame and suffering which the errors of His followers bring upon us. We will endure offences which the early Saints would have marvelled at, and Martyrs would have died to redress. We will work with zeal, but as to the Lord and not to men; recollecting that even Apostles saw the sins of the Churches they planted; that St. Paul predicted that "evil men and seducers would wax worse and worse;" and that St. John seems even to consider extraordinary unbelief as the very sign of the times of the Gospel, as if the light increased the darkness of those who hated it. "Little children, it is the last time; and as ye have heard that Antichrist shall come, even now are there many Antichrists, whereby we know that it is the last time."[97]

Therefore we will seek within for the Epiphany of Christ. We will look towards His holy Altar, and approach it for the fire of love and purity which there burns. We will find comfort in the illumination which Baptism gives. We will rest and be satisfied in His ordinances and in His word. We will bless and praise His name, whenever He vouchsafes to display His glory to us in the chance-meeting of any of His Saints, and we will ever pray Him to manifest it in our own souls.

---

[97] 2 Tim. 3:13; 1 John 2:18

EPIPHANY

The Season of Epiphany

"This beginning of miracles did Jesus in Cana of Galilee, and manifested forth His glory; and His disciples believed on Him."
John 2:11.

The Epiphany is a season especially set apart for adoring the glory of Christ. The word may be taken to mean the manifestation of His glory, and leads us to the contemplation of Him as a King upon His throne in the midst of His court, with His servants around Him, and His guards in attendance. At Christmas we commemorate His grace; and in Lent His temptation; and on Good Friday His sufferings and death; and on Easter Day His victory; and on Holy Thursday His return to the Father; and in Advent we anticipate His second coming. And in all of these seasons He does something, or suffers something: but in the Epiphany and the weeks after it, we celebrate Him, not as on His field of battle, or in His solitary retreat, but as an august and glorious King; we view Him as the Object of our worship. Then only, during His whole earthly history, did He fulfil the type of Solomon, and held (as I may say) a court, and received the homage of His subjects; viz. when He was an infant. His throne was His undefiled Mother's arms; His chamber of state was a cottage or a cave; the worshippers were the wise men of the East, and they brought presents, gold, frankincense, and myrrh. All around and about Him seemed of earth, except to the eye of faith; one note alone had He of Divinity. As great men of this world are often plainly dressed, and look like other men, all but as having some one costly ornament on their breast or on their brow; so the Son of Mary in His lowly dwelling, and in an infant's form, was declared to be the Son of God Most High, the Father of Ages, and the Prince of Peace, by His star; a wonderful appearance which had guided the wise men all the way from the East, even unto Bethlehem.

This being the character of this Sacred Season, our services throughout it, as far as they are proper to it, are full of the image of a king in his royal court, of a sovereign surrounded by subjects, of a glorious prince upon a throne. There is no thought of war, or of strife, or of suffering, or of triumph, or of vengeance connected with the Epiphany, but of august majesty, of power, of prosperity, of splendour, of serenity, of benignity. Now, if at any time, it is fit to say, "The Lord is in His holy temple, let all the earth keep silence before Him."[98] "The Lord sitteth above the waterflood, and the Lord remaineth a king for ever." "The Lord of Hosts is with us; the God of Jacob is our refuge." "O come, let us worship, and fall down, and kneel before the Lord our Maker." "O magnify the Lord our God, and fall down before His footstool, for He is Holy." "O worship the Lord in the beauty of holiness; bring presents, and come into His courts."[99]

I said that at this time of year the portions of our services which are proper to the season are of a character to remind us of a king on his throne, receiving the devotion of his subjects. Such is the narrative itself, already referred to, of the coming of

---

[98] Hab. 2:20
[99] Psalm 29:10; 46:7; 95:6; 99:5; 96:8

the wise men, who sought Him with their gifts from a place afar off, and fell down and worshipped Him. Such too, is the account of His baptism, which forms the Second Lesson of the feast of the Epiphany, when the Holy Ghost descended on Him, and a Voice from heaven acknowledged Him to be the Son of God. And if we look at the Gospels read throughout the season, we shall find them all containing some kingly action of Christ, the Mediator between God and man. Thus in the Gospel for the First Sunday, He manifests His glory in the temple at the age of twelve years, sitting among the doctors, and astonishing them with His wisdom. In the Gospel for the Second Sunday He manifests His glory at the wedding feast, when He turned the water into wine, a miracle not of necessity or urgency, but especially an august and bountiful act—the act of a King, who out of His abundance gave a gift to His own, therewith to make merry with their friends. In the Third Sunday, the leper worships Christ, who thereupon heals him; the centurion, again, reminds Him of His Angels and ministers, and He speaks the word, and his servant is restored forthwith. In the Fourth, a storm arises on the lake, while He is peacefully sleeping, without care or sorrow, on a pillow; then He rises and rebukes the winds and the sea, and a calm follows, deep as that of His own soul, and the beholders worship Him. And next He casts out Legion, after the man possessed with it had also "run and worshipped Him."[100] In the Fifth, we hear of His kingdom on earth, and of the enemy sowing tares amid the good

---

[100] Mark 5:6

seed. And in the Sixth, of His second Epiphany from heaven, "with power and great glory."

Such is the series of manifestations which the Sundays after the Epiphany bring before us. When He is with the doctors in the temple, He is manifested as a prophet—in turning the water into wine, as a priest—in His miracles of healing, as a bounteous Lord, giving out of His abundance—in His rebuking the sea, as a Sovereign, whose word is law—in the parable of the wheat and tares, as a guardian and ruler—in His second coming, as a lawgiver and judge.

And as in these Gospels we hear of our Saviour's greatness, so in the Epistles and First Lessons we hear of the privileges and the duties of the new people, whom He has formed to show forth His praise. Christians are at once the temple of Christ, and His worshippers and ministers *in* the temple; they are the Bride of the Lamb taken collectively, and taken individually, they are the friends of the Bridegroom and the guests at the marriage feast. In these various points of view are they presented to us in the Services during these weeks. In the Lessons from the prophet Isaiah we read of the gifts and privileges, the characteristics, the power, the fortunes of the Church—how widely spreading, even throughout all the Gentiles; how awful and high, how miraculously endowed, how revered, how powerful upon earth, how rich in temporal goods, how holy, how pure in doctrine, how full of the Spirit. And in the Epistles for the successive Sundays, we hear of the duties and distinguishing marks of her true members, principally as laid down in the twelfth and thirteenth chapters of St. Paul to the Romans; then as the same Apostle enjoins them upon the Colossians; and then in St. John's exhortations in his General Epistle.

The Collects are of the same character, as befit the supplications of subjects coming before their King. The first is for knowledge and power, the second is for peace, the third is for strength in our infirmities, the fourth is for help in temptation, the fifth is for protection, and the sixth is for preparation and purification against Christ's second coming. There is none which would suit a season of trial, or of repentance, or of waiting, or of exultation—they befit a season of peace, thanksgiving, and adoration, when Christ is not manifested in pain, conflict, or victory, but in the tranquil possession of His kingdom.

It will be sufficient to make one reflection, which suggests itself from what I have been saying.

You will observe, then, that the only display of royal greatness, the only season of majesty, homage, and glory, which our Lord had on earth, was in His infancy and youth. Gabriel's message to Mary was in its style and manner such as befitted an Angel speaking to Christ's Mother. Elisabeth, too, saluted Mary, and the future Baptist his hidden Lord, in the same honourable way. Angels announced His birth, and the shepherds worshipped. A star appeared, and the wise men rose from the East and made Him offerings. He was brought to the temple, and Simeon took Him in His arms, and returned thanks for Him. He grew to twelve years old, and again He appeared in the temple, and took His seat in the midst of the doctors. But here His earthly majesty had its end, or if seen afterwards, it was but now and then, by glimpses and by sudden gleams, but with no steady sustained light, and no diffused radiance. We are told at the close of the last-mentioned narrative, "And He went down with His parents, and came to Nazareth, *and was subjected unto them.*"[101] His subjection and servitude now began in fact. He had come in the form of a servant, and now He took on Him a servant's office. How much is contained in the idea of His subjection! and it began, and His time of glory ended, when He was twelve years old.

Solomon, the great type of the Prince of Peace, reigned forty years, and his name and greatness was known far and wide through the East. Joseph, the much-loved son of Jacob, who in an earlier age of the Church, was a type of Christ in His kingdom, was in power and favour eighty years, twice as long as Solomon. But Christ, the true Revealer of secrets, and the Dispenser of the bread of life, the true wisdom and majesty of the Father, manifested His glory but in His early years, and then the Sun of Righteousness was clouded. For He was not to reign really, till He left the world. He has reigned ever since; nay, reigned *in* the world, though He is not in sensible presence in it—the invisible King of a visible kingdom—for He came on earth but to show what His reign would be, after He had left it, and to submit to suffering and dishonour, that He *might* reign.

---

[101] Luke 2:51

It often happens, that when persons are in serious illnesses, and in delirium in consequence, or other disturbance of mind, they have some few minutes of respite in the midst of it, when they are even more than themselves, as if to show us what they really are, and to interpret for us what else would be dreary. And again, some have thought that the minds of children have on them traces of something more than earthly, which fade away as life goes on, but are the promise of what is intended for them hereafter. And somewhat in this way, if we may dare compare ourselves with our gracious Lord, in a parallel though higher way, Christ descends to the shadows of this world, with the transitory tokens on Him of that future glory into which He could not enter till He had suffered. The star burned brightly over Him for awhile, though it then faded away.

We see the same law, as it may be called, of Divine Providence in other cases also. Consider, for instance, how the prospect of our Lord's passion opens upon the Apostles in the sacred history. Where did they hear of it? "Moses and Elias on the mountain appeared with Him in glory, and spake of His decease, which He should accomplish at Jerusalem."[102] That is, the season of His bitter trial was preceded by a short gleam of the glory which was to be, when He was suddenly transfigured, "and the fashion of His countenance was altered, and His raiment was white and glistering."[103] And with this glory in prospect, our Lord abhorred not

---

[102] Luke 9:30-31
[103] Luke 9:29

to die: as it is written, "Who for the joy that was set before Him, endured the Cross, despising the shame."

Again, He forewarned His Apostles that they in like manner should be persecuted for righteousness' sake, and be afflicted and delivered up, and hated and killed. Such was to be their life in this world, "that if in this world only they had had hope in Christ, they had been of all men most miserable."[104] Well then, observe, their trial too was preceded by a season of peace and pleasantness, in anticipation of their future reward; for before the day of Pentecost, for forty days Christ was with them, soothing, comforting, confirming them, "and speaking of the things pertaining unto the kingdom of God."[105] As Moses stood on the mount and saw the promised land and all its riches, and yet Joshua had to fight many battles before he got possession, so did the Apostles, before descending into the valley of the shadow of death, whence nought of heaven was to be seen, stand upon the heights, and look over that valley, which they had to cross, to the city of the living God beyond it.

And so again, St. Paul, after many years of toil, refers back to a time when he had a celestial vision, anticipatory of what was to be his blessedness in the end. "I knew a man in Christ," he says, meaning himself, "about fourteen years ago, caught up to the third heaven... And I knew such a man... how that he was caught up into Paradise, and heard unspeakable

---

[104] 1 Cor. 15:19
[105] Acts 1:3

words, which it is not lawful for a man to utter."[106] St. Paul then, as the twelve Apostles, and as our Lord before him, had his brief season of repose and consolation before the battle.

And lastly: the whole Church also may be said to have had a similar mercy vouchsafed to it at first, in anticipation of what is to be in the end. We know, alas, too well, that, according to our Lord's account of it, tares are to be with the wheat, fish of every kind in the net, all through its sojourning on earth. But in the end, "the saints shall stand before the throne of God, and serve Him day and night in His temple: and the Lamb shall feed them, and shall lead them unto living fountains of waters," and there shall be no more "sorrow nor pain, nor any thing that defileth or worketh abomination," "for without are dogs, and sorcerers, and whore-mongers, and murderers, and idolaters, and whosoever loveth and maketh a lie." Now was not this future glory shadowed forth in that infancy of the Church, when before the seal of the new dispensation was opened and trial began, "there was silence in heaven for half an hour;" and "the disciples continued daily with one accord in the temple, and in prayers, breaking bread from house to house, being of one heart, and of one soul, eating their meat with gladness and singleness of heart, praising God, and having favour with all the people;"[107] while hypocrites and "liars," like Ananias and Sapphira, were struck

---

[106] 2 Cor. 12:3-4
[107] Acts 2:46-47

dead, and "sorcerers," like Simon, were detected and denounced?

To conclude; let us thankfully cherish all seasons of peace and joy which are vouchsafed us here below. Let us beware of abusing them, and of resting in them, of forgetting that they *are* special privileges, of neglecting to look out for trouble and trial, as our due and our portion. Trial is our portion here—we must not think it strange when trial comes after peace. Still God mercifully does grant a respite now and then; and perhaps He grants it to us the more, the more careful we are not to abuse it. For all seasons we must thank Him, for time of sorrow and time of joy, time of warfare and time of peace. And the more we thank Him for the one, the more we shall be drawn to thank Him for the other. Each has its own proper fruit, and its own peculiar blessedness. Yet our mortal flesh shrinks from the one, and of itself prefers the other;— it prefers rest to toil, peace to war, joy to sorrow, health to pain and sickness. When then Christ gives us what is pleasant, let us take it as a refreshment by the way, that we may, when God calls, go in the strength of that meat forty days and forty nights unto Horeb, the mount of God. Let us rejoice in Epiphany with trembling, that at Septuagesima we may go into the vineyard with the labourers with cheerfulness, and may sorrow in Lent with thankfulness; let us rejoice now, not as if we have attained, but in hope of attaining. Let us take our present happiness, not as our true rest, but, as what the land of Canaan was to the Israelites,—a type and shadow of it. If we now enjoy God's ordinances, let us not cease to pray that they may prepare us for His presence hereafter. If we enjoy the presence of friends, let them remind us of the communion of saints before His throne. Let us trust in nothing here, yet draw hope from every thing—that at length the Lord may be our everlasting light, and the days of our mourning may be ended.

Omnipotence in Bonds

"And He went down with them, and came to Nazareth; and was subject to them." Luke 2:51.

At this Christmas season, when we are celebrating those joyful mysteries which ushered in the Gospel, it seems almost an officious intrusion upon our holiday to engage in any exercise of the reason, even though it be in order to enliven the devotional feelings proper to the holy tide. It is a time of religious rest and spiritual festivity, and even on the ground that discussion is a kind of labour, we seem to have a right to be protected against it. And yet, as the days go on, and thankfulness has had free current and joy has had its fill, it seems allowable too, to look back at length on what has been occupying the heart, and to reason upon it. Nay, we seem to have the highest of possible authorities for doing so; for after two of the joyful mysteries, the third and the fifth, the holy Virgin is said to have done this very thing. Upon the Nativity of our Lord and Saviour, the very feast we have been celebrating, the Evangelist tells us, "Mary kept all these words, *pondering* them in her heart"; and after she had found Him in the Temple in the midst of the Doctors, which is the subject of this day's Gospel, "His Mother," we are told, "kept all these words in her heart." Surely, then, it is permitted to me, consistently with the love and adoration due to this happy time of Christmas, to direct your minds, my Brethren, to a consideration which it suggests, not indeed very recondite, on the contrary, obvious to all of us, lying on the very face of the great Mystery, but adapted, I think, both to strengthen the faith and to deepen the love, with which we receive it into our hearts.

"The Word was made flesh, and dwelt among us;" this is the glorious, unsearchable, incomprehensible Truth, on which all our hopes for the future depend, and which we have now been commemorating. It is the wonderful Economy of Redemption, by which God became man, the Highest became the lowest, the Creator took His place among His own creatures, Power became weakness, and Wisdom looked to men like folly. He that was rich was made poor; the Lord of all was rejected: "He came unto His own, and His own received Him not." This, I say, is the grand mystery of the season, and this is the subject on which I now propose to make one remark.

I say then, my Brethren, consider what the Divine Being is, and what we mean, when we use His name. The very first idea of Him, if we make the Creed our guide, is Omnipotence: "I believe in God, the Father Almighty." And if you wish to enter into this idea of Omnipotence, and investigate what it is, trace it back into the further mystery of a past eternity. For ages innumerable, for infinite periods, long and long before any creature existed, He was. When there was no creature to exercise His power upon, still He was Omnipotent in His very Essence, as being not sovereign merely, but sole,—as the One Being, without any greater, less, or equal, full of all resources within, and in need of nothing, and, though infinitely one, yet being, at the same time, a whole infinite universe, as I may say, in Himself;—so much so that the breadth and depth and richness and variety and splendour of this created world which we behold, is simply nothing at all, compared to the vastness of that Ocean of perfection which lay concentrated in the intensity of His unity. A king of this world, though a sovereign, though an autocrat, depends on his subjects; but the Almighty God is absolutely and utterly free from any necessary alliance with His creatures. He is complete in Himself, for this reason, if for no other, that He existed for everlasting ages before any one of them was, and was able to do without them for a past eternity, and then created them all out of nothing. He borrows nothing from them; He owes nothing whatever even to the highest of them; they, on the contrary, owe it to Him that they are even able to remain in their own proper nature, and they derive from Him, moment by moment, every pulsation of their life and every ray of such glory as they possess.

Such is the omnipotent, self-dependent God: fixed in His own centre, and needing no point of motion or vantage-ground out of Himself, whereupon to bring into action, or to use, or to apply, His inexhaustible power. He can make, He can unmake; He can decree and bring to pass, He can direct, control, and resolve, absolutely according to His will. He could create this vast material world, with all its suns and globes, and its illimitable spaces, in a moment. All its overwhelming multiplicity of laws, and complexity of formations, and intricacy of contrivances, both to originate and to accomplish, is with Him but the work of a moment. He could destroy it all in all its parts in a moment; in the same one moment He could create another universe instead of it, indefinitely more vast, more beautiful, more marvellous, and indefinitely unlike that universe which He was annihilating. He could bring into existence and destroy an infinite series of such universes, each in succession more perfect than that which immediately preceded it. He is the Creator, too, of all the intellectual natures which exist, whether in the heavens above, or on the earth, or in the regions under the earth. Angels in their nine multitudinous orders, and men in their populous generations, good spirits and bad, saints and souls on trial, the saved and the lost, first, He created them and creates, each in its own time; and next, He keeps the complete and exact tale of them all, as He keeps the catalogue also of all the beasts, the birds, the fishes, the reptiles, and insects, all over the earth. Not a sparrow falls without Him; not a hair of our heads, but He has counted it in with the rest; and so, too, not a soul, but He has before Him its whole history from beginning to end, and its every thought, word, and deed, and its every motion through every day, and its relative place in the scale of merit and of sin.

And, while He thus intermingles His presence and His operations with an ineffable intimacy of union in every place, in every substance, in every act, everywhere, He is at the same time, as I have said, infinitely separated from everything, and absolutely incommunicable and unapproachable, and self-dependent in His own glorious Essence. Nothing can add to Him; no one can be His creditor, no one can claim anything of Him. He has no duties (if I may use such a term) towards the beings He has created. It is a saying about earthly possessions, that property has its duties as well as its privileges. Such words and such ideas apply not to the Self-subsisting, Everlasting God. He asks of His creatures, "Is it not lawful for Me to do what I will?" And St. Paul says of Him: "O man! who art thou that repliest against God? shall the thing formed say to Him who formed it, Why hast Thou made me thus?" If I must still use the word "duties" or obligations of Almighty God, I will say, that He has obligations towards Himself, but none towards us. What binds Him is the dictate of His own holy and perfect attributes. He is just and true, because His attributes are such; but we have no claims upon Him. Or, if we have claims, it is in consequence of His own gratuitous and express promise, by which indeed He does bind Himself; and then He is but faithful to His own word, because He is the Truth, and His obligation is still to Himself, and not to us. You know, my Brethren, we, in our turn, have no duties toward the brute creation; there is no relation of justice between them and us. Of course we are bound not to treat them ill, for cruelty is an offence against that holy Law which our Maker has written on our hearts, and is displeasing to Him. But *they* can claim nothing at our hands; into our hands they are absolutely delivered. We may use them, we may destroy them at our pleasure, not our wanton pleasure, but still for our own ends, for our own benefit or satisfaction, provided we can give a rational account of what we do. Now, I do not say that the case is the same between us and our Maker, but it is illustrated by this parallel. He has no account at all to render to us: He has no claims of ours to settle: we are bound to Him; He is not bound to us, except as He binds Himself: we have no merit in His sight, and can do Him no service, unless His promise brings these ideas into existence. I say, He is only bound by His own perfect Nature, infinitely good, and holy, and true, as it is; and in that is the creature's stay. If we accuse Him, He will prevail, according to the text, "that Thou mayest be justified in Thy words, and mayest overcome when Thou art judged." And if we are utterly without claims upon Him as creatures, we are doubly destitute considered as sinners also: and thus, if even Angels are unprofitable in His sight, what are we?

In the words of Holy Scripture: "Can a man be compared with God? What doth it profit God, if thou be just? or what dost thou give Him, if thy way be unspotted? Behold, even the moon doth not shine, and the stars are not pure in His sight. Behold, among His saints, none is unchangeable, and the heavens are not pure in His sight. Behold, they that serve Him are not steadfast, and in His Angels He found wickedness. How much more is man abominable and unprofitable, who drinketh iniquity like water! Behold, He taketh away, and who can hinder Him? Who will say to Him: What dost Thou? Why dost thou strive against Him? for He giveth not account of any of His matters."[108]

Such is the Omnipotence, the Self-dependence, the Self-sufficiency, the infinite Liberty of the Eternal God, our Creator and Judge. And now, this being so, let me go on to the particular thought which I wish, my Brethren, to suggest to you for your reflection at this season.

---

[108] cf. Job, cap. 4, 9, 15, 22, 25, 33

It is, not merely that God became man, not merely that the All-possessing became destitute; but the point on which I shall particularly insist is, in contrast with what I have been enlarging on, that the All-powerful, the All-free, the Infinite, became and becomes, as the text says, "subject" to the creature; nay, not only a subject, but literally a captive, a prisoner, and that not once, but on many different occasions and in many different ways.

Now, observe, my Brethren, when the Eternal son of God came among us, He might have taken our nature, as Adam received it, from the earth, and have begun His human life at mature age; He might have been moulded under the immediate hand of the Creator; He need have known nothing of the feebleness of infancy or the slow growth of manhood. This might have been, had He so willed; but no: He preferred the penance of taking His place in the line of Adam, and of being born of a woman. This was the very scandal of the ancient heretics, as it has been of free-thinkers in all ages. They shrank from the notion of such a birth from Mary, as a something simply intolerable and past belief; and truly in that belief is the commencement of the wonderful captivity of the Infinite God, on which I am to dwell. Yet I will not do more than suggest so much of it to your devout meditation. I mean the long imprisonment He had, before His birth, in the womb of the Immaculate Mary. There was He in His human nature, who, as God, is everywhere; there was He, as regards His human soul, conscious from the first with a full intelligence, and feeling the extreme irksomeness of the prison-house, full of grace as it was.

At length He sees the light, and He is free; but free only in that His imprisonment is changed. The very first act of His Mother's on His birth, is both an example and a figure of His life-long captivity. "Mary brought forth her first-born Son, and wrapped Him up in swaddling clothes, and laid Him in a manger." It is the custom in those southern parts to treat the new-born babe in a way strange to this age and country. The infant is swathed around with cloths much resembling the winding-sheet, the bandages and ligaments of the dead. You may recollect, my Brethren, the account of Lazarus's revival; how that, when miracle had lifted him up out of the tomb, there he lay motionless, till his fastenings were cut off from him. "He that had been dead came forth, bound foot and hand with winding-bands; and Jesus said to them: Loose him, and let him go." So was it with that wonder-working Lord Himself in His own infancy. He submitted to the customs, as well as to the ritual, of His nation; and, as He had lain so long in Mary's womb, so now again He left that sacred prison, only that her loving hands might manacle and fetter Him once more, inflicting on Him the special penance which He had chosen. And so, like some inanimate image of wood or stone, the All-powerful lies in the manger, or on her bosom, doubly helpless, both because His infancy is feeble, and because His bonds are strong.

It is in this wise He was shown to the shepherds; thus He was worshipped by the wise men; thus He was presented in the Temple, taken up in Simeon's arms, hurried off to Egypt by night, His tender Mother adoring the while that abject captivity to which it was her awful duty to reduce Him. So His first months passed; and though, as time went on, He grew in stature, and burst His bonds, still through a slow and tedious advance did He enter on His adolescence. And then, when for a moment He anticipated His mission and sat down among the Doctors in the Temple, He was quickly recalled by His Mother's chiding, and went back again to her and Joseph, and, in the emphatic words of the text, was "subject unto them." It is said, He worked at His father's trade, not even yet His own master, and confined till the age of thirty to the limits of one city.

And when at length the hour came for His breaking away from His humble home and quitting Nazareth, even then this law of captivity, as I may call it, continued, and that even with the circumstances of a frightful development. For is it not terrifying, so as even to scare the mind, that in His infancy indeed His Mother's pure embrace had been His prison, but now, as a preparation for His public ministry, He is made over to His enemy, and undergoes the handling of the foul spirit himself! The rebel archangel, who would *not* be in subjection, who had assailed the throne of God, and had been cast out of heaven, he it is who now has got fast hold of the Eternal Word Incarnate, and is lifting Him up, and transporting Him according to his will; taking Him into the holy city, and setting Him upon the pinnacle of the Temple, and taking Him up into a very high mountain in order to seduce Him with a bribe of the unshackled lordship of the wide earth. "What concord hath Christ with Belial?" Yet the fiend is allowed the momentary possession of the Omnipotent.

But at least when He has begun to preach, He will be free. My Brethren, it is true; but even then the threatenings at least and the earnests of a renewed captivity pursue Him. As soon as He does miracles and collects followers, His brethren take the alarm, and try to capture Him. "When His friends had heard of it, they went out to lay hold of Him, for they said, He is become mad." When He preached in Nazareth, "the people rose and seized Him violently, and brought Him to the brow of the hill, to cast Him headlong." At another time He was in danger from His own hearers; they went about to take Him by force to make Him a king. At another time, "the Scribes and Pharisees sent ministers to apprehend Him." At another time, Herod was about to seize Him and put Him to death.

At length He is to die for us; but still that sacrifice of Himself was not to please Him, if imprisonment was away. He allowed Himself, in the Church's words, "manibus tradi nocentium"—*to be given into the hands of the violent*.[109] Now, I ask, what need of this superfluity of humiliation? He was to shed His blood and die; doubtless: but in the manifold dispositions of Providence there were many ways whereby to die, without falling into the fierce handling of jailers and hangmen. He might have taken upon Himself the mode of satisfying the Divine Decree, and have

---

[109] cf. The Way of the Cross prayers

dispensed with the instrumentality of man. We read in history of kings going to death, who refused the assistance of the executioner, and submitted to their fate by their own act. And it was in order to remind us that He *need* not have undergone that profanation, that, on His enemies first approaching Him, He smote them to the ground. And again, it was in order to impress upon us that He *did* undergo it, that He touchingly asked them: "Are ye come out as to a robber, with swords and clubs, to apprehend Me? but this is your hour and the power of darkness."

Thus He spoke, and that expostulation was the immediate signal for those special indignities to begin in which He chose to invest His passion and death. He who was submitted to the wine-press in Gethsemani, and agonized with none to see Him but Apostles and attendant Angels, might surely have gone through His solemn sacrifice in solitude, as He commenced it; but He preferred the "hands of men"; He preferred the loathsome kiss of the traitor; He preferred the staves and swords of the ministers of a fallen priesthood; He preferred to die in the midst of a furious mob, haling Him to and fro; under the fists and scourges and hammers of savage lictors; now shut up in a dungeon, now dragged before the judgment-seat, now tied to a pillar, now nailed to the cross, and then at length, when the worst was over, and His soul was fled, hurried, as the best His friends could do for Him, hurried into a narrow sepulchre of stone. O marvellous dispensation, full of mystery! that the God of Nature, the Lord of the Universe, should take to Himself a body to suffer and die in; not only so, but should not even allow

Himself the birthright of man, should refuse to be master of His own limbs, and outgrow the necessity of a Mother's arms, only to present Himself to the tyrannous grasp of the heathen soldiers.

And now surely, my Brethren, we are come to the end of these wonders. He tore open the solid rock; He rose from the tomb; He ascended on high; He is far off from the earth; He is safe from profanation; and the soul and body, which He assumed, partake of course, as far as created nature allows, of the Sovereign Freedom and the Independence of Omnipotence. It is not so: He is indeed beyond the reach of suffering; but you anticipate, my Brethren, what I have yet to say. Is He then so enamoured of the prison, that He should purpose to revisit earth again, in order that, as far as possible, He may undergo it still? Does He set such a value on subjection to His creatures, that, before He goes away, on the very eve of His betrayal, He must actually make provision, after death, for perpetuating His captivity to the end of the world? My Brethren, the great truth is daily before our eyes: He has ordained the standing miracle of His Body and Blood under visible symbols, that He may secure thereby the standing mystery of Omnipotence in bonds.

He took bread, and blessed, and made it His Body; He took wine, and gave thanks, and made it His Blood; and He gave His priests the power to do what He had done. Henceforth, He is in the hands of sinners once more. Frail, ignorant, sinful man, by the sacerdotal power given to him, compels the presence of the Highest; he lays Him up in a small tabernacle; he dispenses Him to a sinful people. Those who are only just now cleansed from mortal sin, open their lips for Him; those who are soon to return to mortal sin, receive Him into their breasts; those who are polluted with vanity and selfishness and ambition and pride, presume to make Him their guest; the frivolous, the tepid, the worldly-minded, fear not to welcome Him. Alas! alas! even those who wish to be more in earnest, entertain Him with cold and wandering thoughts, and quench that Love which would inflame them with Its own fire, did they but open to It. Such are the best of us; and then for the worst? O my Brethren, what shall we say of sacrilege? of His reception into hearts polluted with mortal, unforsaken sin? of those further nameless profanations, which from time to time occur, when unbelief dares to present itself at the Holy Altar, and blasphemously gains possession of Him?

My Brethren, it is plain that, when we confess God as Omnipotent only, we have gained but a half-knowledge of Him: His is an Omnipotence which can at the same time swathe Itself in infirmity and can become the captive of Its own creatures. He has, if I may so speak, the incomprehensible power of even making Himself weak. We must know Him by His names, Emmanuel and Jesus, to know Him perfectly.

One word more before I conclude. Some persons may consider that a thought, such as that I have been enlarging on, is a difficulty to faith. Every one has his own trials and his own scandals: I grant it. For me, my Brethren, I can only say that its effect on myself lies just in the very opposite direction, and, awful as it is, it does but suggest an incentive, as for adoration, so for faith also. What human teacher could thus open for us an insight into the infinitude of the Divine Counsels? Eye of man hath not seen the face of God; and heart of man could never have conceived or invented so wonderful a manifestation, as the Gospel contains, of His ineffable, overwhelming Attributes. I believe the infinite condescension of the Highest to be true, because it has been imagined. Moreover, I recognize it to be true, just as I believe in the laws of this material world, according as human science elicits them; viz., because I see here the silent operation, beneath the surface, of a great principle, which is not seen till it is investigated. I adore a truth, which, though patent to all who look for it, yet, to be seen in its consistency and symmetry, *has* to be looked for. And further, I glory in it, for I see in it the most awful antagonism to the very idea and essence of sin, whether as existing in Angels or in men. For what was the sin of Lucifer, but the resolve to be his own master? What was the sin of Adam, but impatience of subjection, and a desire to be his own god? What is the sin of all his children, but the movement, not of passion merely, not of selfishness, not of unbelief, but of pride, of the heart rising against the law of God, and set on being emancipated from its trammels? What is the sin of Antichrist, but, as St. Paul says, that of being "the Lawless One," of "opposing or being lifted up against all that is called God, or worshipped, so that he sitteth in the temple of God, showing himself as if he were God"? If, then, the very principle of sin is insubordination, is there not a stupendous meaning in the fact, that He, the Eternal, who alone is sovereign and supreme, has given us an example in His own Person of that love of subjection, which in Him alone is simply voluntary, but in all creatures is an elementary duty?

O my Brethren, let us blush at our own pride and self-will. Let us call to mind our impatience at God's providences towards us, our wayward longings after what cannot be, our headstrong efforts to reverse His just decrees, our bootless conflicts with the stern necessities which hem us in, our irritation at ignorance or suspense about His will, our fierce, passionate wilfulness when we see that will too clearly, our haughty contempt of His ordinances, our determination to do things for ourselves without Him, our preference of our own reason to His word,—the many, many shapes in which the Old Adam shows itself, and one or other of which our conscience tells us is our own; and let us pray Him who is independent of us all, yet who at this season became as though our fellow and our servant, to teach us our place in His wide universe, and to make us ambitious only of that grace here and glory hereafter, which He has purchased for us by His own humiliation.